LETTERS FROM ALEPPO

Chronicles of War and Hope

LETTERS

CHRONICLES OF

FROM

WAR AND HOPE

ALEPPO

BY IBRAHIM ALSABAGH

columba press

First published in 2017 by
columba press
23 Merrion Square
Dublin 2, Ireland
www.columba.ie

Translated from the Italian by Joan Rundo

Reproduced with kind permission by Fondazione Terra Santa, Via Giovanni
Gherardini 5, 20145 Mila, Italy. Copyright for *Un istante prima dell'alba*
reserved by Fondazione Terra Santa.

ISBN: 978-1-78218-323-5

Set in Freight Text Pro 10/14
Cover and book design by Alba Esteban | Columba Press
Cover photography by Ali Hashisho from Reuters
Front and back image: A general view of Aleppo city at dawn,
Syria. February 2, 2017

Printed by Jellyfish Solutions

CONTENTS

INTRODUCTION

On 22 December 2016, a message from Father Ibrahim Alsabagh, a Friar Minor and parish priest in Aleppo, Syria, reached his friends and benefactors in Europe: "After long talks between the army and the armed militia, the military groups have handed over their weapons and are leaving the eastern part of the city. The army has announced that Aleppo can be considered a 'safe city'. As soon as the news arrived, all the mosques called their faithful to celebrate and the churches, the ones that still had their bell tower, rang the bells for a long time. A dream has come true." These are words full of hope; just a few days before Christmas, the liberation of the eastern part of the city "is the best gift possible".

Since then, Aleppo has certainly entered a new phase. There are many hopes and expectations, but the population continues to have enormous needs. After six years of war, hundreds of thousands of dead (apparently more than 300,000, but nobody really knows), more than six million refugees and displaced persons, the situation of Syria and Aleppo is still tragic. Those who left during the bombings of the eastern part of the city live in total poverty.

At this point, we are all wondering: will there be peace in Syria soon? What is awaiting Aleppo? What remains of what was once one of the most beautiful and lively cities in the Middle East? Syria invites us to keep our attention on the tragedy through which it is living. The city, for the time being, is controlled almost entirely by the loyalist army, but there are pockets of resistance. The shooting and the bombings continue: "The war is not over yet," Father Ibrahim points out.

Bashar al-Assad's government has promised to intervene in the productive areas to try and get some modest economic activity started again, to support the population that has remained. The winter of Aleppo (and not only the meteorological one) will last for a long time yet. The city is a spectral agglomeration of bombed houses and streets full of rubble. Unexploded devices are often hidden in the ruins, transforming them into mortal traps.

In this book – updated to reflect recent developments – Father Ibrahim is not concerned about understanding the strategies of the chancelleries or investigating the geopolitical reasons for the Syrian conflict. Bookshops are full of books that attempt to offer interpretations.

In this book, which is profoundly different from all the others on the market, Father Ibrahim tells the story of how people continue to live in Aleppo through the tragedy of the war, how the hope for a better future is fuelled when having hope seems to be a curse and how the sense of life (and death) is recovered in a situation where evil and violence amount to pure stupidity.

These are short notes, fulminating reflections, surges of life, moans and screams that become prayers: suffering in the very flesh of a people. They are waiting for the end of a nightmare, just as, the moment before dawn, light suddenly appears, gloriously announcing the day to come.

A PLEA FROM SYRIA

Msgr Georges Abou Khazen
Apostolic Vicar of Aleppo for the Latins

We need this river of blood to stop, on both sides. Here the human being no longer has any value! But we believe in the strength of prayer and we ask people to pray for peace. It is increasingly urgent to persuade those who are fighting to talk and put down their weapons. The people who are still here in Aleppo, whether Christian or Muslim, live in terror. It always surprises us to see how the faction of the so-called "rebels", which now coincides with the Islamic Caliphate, despite the proclamations, is, in the end, supported by the west. We have no idea of how many Christians are left in the city; those who can, flee. Certainly less than half of the 220,000 who once lived here remain.

The situation in Aleppo is very difficult, not only for obvious safety reasons. There is no electricity. We can only produce it using diesel oil. Fuel is expensive and is not easy to find. Drinking water is scarce. In some districts, it only arrives in cistern tanks and people have to queue with jerry cans and pay for it. Luckily we have wells in the churches and so we can also distribute water. In the meantime people's needs are increasing. There is the problem of the houses that have been destroyed. So we are trying to help those who no longer have a home to find somewhere to live. The price of commodities is sky-high, as is inflation. Then there is growing unemployment, worsened by the economic embargo. We, as the Church, would so much like to help the unemployed to survive, the small artisans to find work. But in front of the unstoppable river of blood, we are asking only for peace. We are counting on your prayers.

Aleppo, September 2016*

*The plea, although made before the rebel militia were chased out of the east of Aleppo, remains very topical. The social picture it outlines is essentially unchanged. Today the fighting in the city may have been drastically reduced, but the conditions of the population remain very difficult. The shortage of water, electricity and work and the difficulties of obtaining provisions continue to mar the existence of the ordinary people. In short, the war is by no means over.

LETTERS

These letters tell of the devastation wrought by the bombings, showing the depth of the horror experienced by Aleppo. The story of a conversation with a mother who has lost her children in war conveys the same message. At the same time, we learn that the distribution of food to those who no longer have any money gives hope. Similarly, a party with games and balloons at the Sunday school helps the smallest children, the first victims of war, to smile again.

In the first section of this book, we have collected the newsletters that Father Ibrahim Alsabagh sends via internet to his Italian friends in order to share his day-by-day experiences in Aleppo with them. His stories manifest, often without commentary, his amazement at what he has just seen or heard, whether tragic or joyous. They are the spontaneous impressions of a Christian who finds himself on the front line of hatred (but also of hope), and tries to give reasons for his faith.

The first newsletter is dated 26 January 2015, just a few weeks after Father Ibrahim arrived in the city. He describes, almost incredulous, the appalling reality in which he landed without warning. From the very beginning, he tells of the first attempts to answer and react to evil. The last newsletter is dated 5 January 2017 and in it he speaks of reconstruction and the future, even though the situation remains critical.

Along with newsletters, the first section of the book includes some articles Father Ibrahim published in the newspaper *Avvenire* (12 October 2015, 23 December 2015), three articles in the supplement *La Porta Aperta* (6 December 2015, 8 May and 9 October 2016) and a letter to the children of the Sunday schools "twinned" with the Sunday school of his parish, St Francis in Aleppo.

Introductory editorial notes serve to help the English-speaking reader contextualise the episodes related.

PART I

At the start of 2015, when Father Ibrahim first arrived in Aleppo, the rebels launched an offensive against the districts held by the regular Syrian army, gaining terrain. The bombings also increased in the area of the Latin parish church, but this did not prevent the friars from continuing their activities: from blessing homes to creating a room where students could study.

26 JANUARY 2015

Until the very last, I hoped to come to Italy as planned, but I couldn't leave the parish with the other brother on his own. This is why I am writing this letter to you, in which I will try to tell you about some aspects of my mission in Aleppo.

Since Christmas, we have had some very difficult times, with bombs and gas bombs[1] falling on homes in our area. Last Thursday, a Catholic church of the Armenian rite was attacked and partially destroyed. The sporadic bombings are destroying several homes, with the inevitable consequence that people have been killed or seriously wounded.

Winter in Aleppo

In Aleppo, this winter's intense cold is dramatically conditioning people's lives. There is hardly any diesel oil and, to render a service to the people, we turn to the civil authorities, now and again obtaining small quantities; the same applies for gas.

Our large church of St Francis is freezing, but the faithful continue to take part in the celebrations with heroic courage. Both of us friars have fallen ill due to the cold. Our colds got worse every time we went down into the church to celebrate Mass and hear confessions; it took a long time for us to get rid of them.

---

1 Home made rockets made up of empty gas tanks filled with explosives and fragments of iron

The charity association

Recently I have started to make some changes to our charity association, a sort of parish Caritas. The renewal consists of replacing the personnel, voluntary and paid, and of changing the criteria for evaluating needs and the practical methods of aid. The sum necessary for the monthly assistance of our poor is growing all the time, while local sources are being exhausted due to general poverty. The number of families and individuals we assist has exceeded 230, but this number is bound to increase rapidly with the new arrivals and requests. After an attentive study of the real needs for these new cases, we can recognise almost immediately that aid has to be given, and straight away.

I am not completely satisfied with our association. We have to improve the standard of organisation to be able to serve a larger number of people. Since my arrival in Aleppo quite a lot has already been done.

The dramatic economic and social situation

The economic situation in Syria is worsening very quickly. A few days ago, the government announced that the price of diesel oil was going up from 85 Syrian pounds to 125 Syrian pounds while, for gas, the price of a tank is going up from 1,100 Syrian pounds to 1,500 Syrian pounds.[2] The same applies to petrol. As a consequence, the cost of bread and all food, including staples, has considerably increased. Some surveys show a continuous collapse of the Syrian pound with respect to the dollar. This implies an increase in poverty. We have to be ready for an increasingly difficult scenario.

It is not difficult to imagine the atmosphere of despair among our people. The elderly ill suffer disproportionately from the cold. Women and children display many symptoms of malnutrition. Families can no

2 At the beginning of the war in 2012, one euro was worth 85 Syrian pounds. In the first few months of 2015, when Father Ibrahim wrote this letter, 400 Syrian pounds were perhaps not enough to buy one euro. In the middle of 2016, depending on the moment, one euro was worth between 500 and 600 Syrian pounds. The devaluation of the currency is one of the negative consequences of the war. At the same time, due to inflation, as Father Ibrahim says, the prices of staple foods shot up. In Aleppo, even those who had accumulated capital see it vanish very quickly and soon end up poor.

longer pay the rent on their homes. Many people, especially those with children, no longer think about looking after their own health and so – also due to minor ailments that remain neglected for a long time – are in very poor health, which can even lead to death.

Some concrete cases

This morning, a couple with five children who are university students came to us. Neither of them can find work. The mother whispered to me that she has an eye disease and that she should have an operation, as she is already starting to lose her sight, but she added that, with the few resources they have left, she prefers to pay the university fees for her children, even if she were to become completely blind or die of hunger.

I discover at least four cases a day of extreme need. Some time ago, an elderly lady came to see me explaining her situation of extreme poverty and illness. Then she showed me a loaded pistol, saying that she was ready to take her own life "in a dignified way" if the pain and her despair got too much to bear. Yesterday, a widow with two children confessed to me that she had not had any gas, diesel oil or electricity for two months, but only a little drinking water. I had to take a tank of gas, which had just been filled from the monastery, and send it immediately to this woman's home.

A reading room for university students

The period of university examinations began on 5 January throughout Syria, so we started an aid project for university students and for those sitting the final school examination. They have no electricity or heating at home. Since the libraries in the different Aleppo churches are now closed due to the lack of diesel oil, I decided to open a reading room in the parish, in the rooms where catechism is taught. It can hold up to 60 students. We furnished the rooms, heating them with an appliance that consumes very little diesel oil, then we opened them for students from 9am to 8pm.

The same project included appointing a young married couple and some unemployed people to be in charge of the reading room. There are 80 students registered for the time being and we ask for only a very small registration fee. In the reading room, there is also the possibility of a hot drink for those who need one. Yesterday, noticing that several of the students did not eat from the morning until the evening, we bought bread and chocolate, offering 32 of them something to eat. It was the best present they could have imagined.

I am very pleased with this concrete service that we can still offer our young people and I hope – if Providence continues to be with us – to make it permanent, not only for the period of exams but throughout the year. I also hope to be able to offer them something to eat every day.

Blessing homes

I started to visit the homes to bless on 13 January. With us, the period of blessing homes starts with the feast of Jesus' baptism.[3] On the first day, I was able to go to six homes and I met various people, including adults, who had not had the sacrament of communion and several elderly people who had not left their homes for years. Many of them expressed their desire and need to receive communion at least once a month. Thanks to these visits, I was able to meet many very poor families and invite them to come to our charity association to receive monthly aid.

I am fighting against time and the countless things which have to be done to keep going out for blessings at least three times a week. But I don't know whether I will be able to continue, due to the commitments of receiving the many people who come to the parish office every day. I am nevertheless tranquil because I believe I don't spare myself. I give the whole of myself and all my energy and resources to my people. My conscience is at peace and I am consoled about everything. I work hard every day from 7am to 11pm, without a break, not even for a short walk. Ours is work which would take 10 people to do, though there are only two of us. However, I am doing no more than my father and my mother offered me for many years and I am happy to be able to give of myself as well, as the father of a much larger family. I feel that imitating the assiduous service my parents gave me helps me along my path to holiness.

3   In the Roman rite, this feast is celebrated on the Sunday after the Epiphany.

24 FEBRUARY 2015

Since my arrival in Aleppo, the flow of those who knock on our door has increased every day. They are mainly families who ask for all sorts of help. My parish desk is covered in many small slips of paper. Each one is a memo for a case or a problem to solve. Lots of people come to the office. There are those who are upset and cry or shout and there are those who complain about the church, sometimes even hurting those who listen to them. They are all welcomed with a smile, very calmly, and we do not let them leave until their hearts are at peace, with a consolation linked with the word of God, some good advice and some material help. After these meetings, we pray fervently until the will of our Lord appears clearly. Only then do we spring into action, in general adopting the best course to take and the person is perfectly convinced. We often have to call the same person several times to discuss new possibilities or learn more about the situation through other questions.

Receiving people or visiting families?

I will not conceal that, in our missionary activity, we are torn between receiving people and visiting families. When we go out for visits, the desire arises in us not to go back to the monastery. We remember the life of Jesus, his public mission amid the people in the squares: praying, teaching, healing and casting out demons. Our heart wants to remain with Jesus and do what he did. But how can we neglect the crowds that come knocking on the monastery door every day? Here, too, they have to be able to meet Jesus who gives himself to his children to listen to them, speak to them and guide them. What is to be done? Go out or stay in the monastery to receive the people who come? Unlike last month, in the past few days we have been choosing to receive visitors. There is actually a serious impediment to our visits: the bombs falling thickly and suddenly, which unfortunately spare nobody.

How we spend our day

The day starts with Mass at 7.30am. While one friar celebrates, the other hears confessions. Immediately after the celebration, we go up into the monastery chapel to pray the divine office: both lauds and midday prayer. We pray calmly, respecting all the spaces of silence. These moments, more than any other, give us the strength to carry on. We have found that this is the best arrangement to be able to pray together, as work never leaves us free time until late in the evening. Vespers are recited individually. After almost an hour of intense prayer together in the chapel we have breakfast while discussing our appointments. Then in the parish office the race begins for the many things to do and the bell begins to ring much earlier than the time established for receiving visitors. We stop at around one for a short lunch break. We take advantage of this time to discuss the various situations of the people who have come to see us. We go back to the office to deal with the commitments in our schedule or to do work that requires special concentration.

At 3.30pm the visits begin again and at 4.50pm we are back in the basilica. Once again, while one friar hears confessions, the other celebrates the eucharist. After this, the meetings start again, both in the office and with the parish groups. At 8pm, the reading room for the students also closes. When everyone has left and the monastery is closed, we have dinner, updating each other on the people we have seen, the problems and all the decisions and jobs for the next day.

After dinner, we often go back to the office to work on jobs that we had not been able to complete during the day. The silence is often interrupted by bombing or shooting. At the end of the day, if there is water, hot or not, we have a shower, exhausted. After our personal prayers, we entrust ourselves to the Spirit of the Lord and finally go to bed.

We are considering praying vespers in Arabic in the church of St Francis after the evening Mass with the parishioners who wish to do so. We hope that we will be able to do this and not to lose the gift of celebrating vespers with the community.

There are more and more funerals

This February is the month of Sister Death. We have seen many – too many – funerals. And the number is rising. They are the elderly and ill who cannot resist the cold and malnutrition. Most of the deceased are poor. One priest confided in me that these people die more out of despair than of cold or hunger. When they no longer have electricity, diesel oil, water or food, the poor let themselves go, dying in anguish.

Filling in the gaps in assistance offered by other associations

There are many families who live in rented property and can no longer pay their monthly rent. They live in precarious situations, on the borderline of subsistence. When they call asking us to visit them, we see their poverty first-hand, especially if they have a lot of children.

Some ecclesiastical associations that help our families pay part of their rent require do so on condition that there is a legal contract. But only a few landlords accept one, with the result that many families in need are not helped. We are trying to intervene as we best can, filling in these gaps with concrete support.

What's more, the list of operations covered by these charitable associations does not include those considered non-essential, but these can be urgent and necessary, such as operations on the eyes or teeth. We try to take on these cases as well.

Support for university students

Christian Syrian families are ready to make sacrifices of food or health, but they will not sacrifice the education of their children. They enrol them in private Christian schools because the state schools are in a state of abject poverty and total deterioration; this applies both to primary and secondary schools and to the universities.

We are helping about 100 young university students who attend both state and private universities. Most of them are aware of the risk of not being able to continue their studies due to lack of money, but this does not reduce their commitment and their concentration. This month, we gave each of them about 20 euro. The figure is only enough to pay for daily travel expenses to and from the university and for a few cups of coffee over a month, but what counts is that the church is perceived as being concretely present in the main concern of families: the future of their children. If only we could, we would without a doubt contribute much more to all our schoolchildren and university students, as support from the church for the hope for Syria's future.

The banks are asking for the payment of mortgages

Another difficulty, and one that is not of little import, has been added to the list of those already faced by families: monthly repayments of mortgages taken out with the banks years ago, when families decided to buy a home. Since the start of the war in the country, many families are no longer in a position to pay. In the past few days, banks have issued orders for the amounts that have accumulated over the years to be repaid. They are threatening court proceedings, which could easily result in a ruling of eviction, seizure and sale of homes. There are enormous sums at stake and some families have begun to ask for help, although in only a few cases. We have tried to meet these requests, aware that many will unfortunately remain without support.

Difficulties with food aid

Yesterday I compared the food package we distribute with the one offered by other associations; ours is poorer. We have to add nourishing food for children, such as milk and tins of tuna.

Oil, which was a very common product in Syria (poured onto bread; it was the food of the poor), is scarce today and therefore very expensive. We relied on the package of the Red Crescent[4] distributed by the government every 50 days. We received it last this month, but we have been told that as of today it will be given every four or eight months. We will have to get ready for this as well, buying everything at our own expense.

The start of Lent in the reading room

The end of the period of exams coincides with the start of Lent. After the Mass at 7.30pm, I went down to the reading room for university students to celebrate the eucharist with some of them. With the electricity switched off, everything took place by candlelight. As an altar, we used a desk, to show the importance of offering the Lord the commitment of the youngsters who come to this room every day. We remembered and gave thanks for all those who had finished their exams and those who were unable to take part in the celebration.

A few days before the start of Lent, I met several youngsters who come

4 In Arab countries the Red Crescent is the equivalent of the Red Cross.

to the reading room. They expressed their gratitude to me. During the Mass of Ash Wednesday, I saw this gratitude shine in their eyes. Without a doubt, this is addressed to the Lord, the beginning of all good. We friars are only "unworthy servants" (Lk 17:10), nothing more.

The via crucis of the first Friday of Lent

As is traditional in Aleppo as well, for the faithful of the Latin rite we celebrated the via crucis of the first Friday of Lent on 20 February in the basilica of St Francis. We adopted the same text as Jerusalem, to experience this important moment in communion with our brothers of the Custody of the Holy Land. At the end of the via crucis, we prayed with all our heart for everyone who supports us from afar so that we can continue our mission in this devastated city.

PART II

In mid-February, the Syrian army launched an offensive on the territory north of Aleppo, winning several villages. However, a counter-offensive by the rebels a few days later forced the government troops to retreat. This also explains the intensification of the bombings in the area of Aleppo where the parish is.

3 MARCH 2015

The shower of bombs continues to fall on Aleppo, affecting our area of Azizieh as well. People are frightened to come to church so, for the past few days, the number of faithful has decreased considerably. There was talk for a long time of a truce, but this seems to have disappeared without a trace; the shootings and the bombings of inhabited areas have increased. Nevertheless, we try, as far as possible, to continue the catechism meetings, in particular those in preparation for the first communion and for confirmation.

Last Sunday, during Mass, we prayed for the dead, the injured and the families whose houses had been destroyed in the latest bombings. This prayer, however, must not be our only response. We warmly invite all the faithful to react, through solidarity and charity, by going to visit the people and the houses that have been hit, praying with those who are oppressed and saddened and giving everything possible to relieve their suffering. We Christians of Aleppo should not be passive, but active, offering our charity tangibly and immediately. Lastly, we should never allow doubt and despair to prevail.

Aleppo, a devastated city

Words are not enough to describe the reality of Aleppo. It is a city that has been destroyed.

One day, a priest, comparing what is happening in Syria with the civil war in Lebanon,[5] said to me: "It's true that in Lebanon we were under fire, in the middle of the war, from door to door, but we kept on working; there was work. The problem with the war in Syria, especially in Aleppo, is that people have lost their jobs. The devastation led to the destruction of basic resources and industries."

We are witnessing an economic catastrophe, a collapse of the whole of society, of a people and of a culture. In the middle of this disaster, we, as the church, try to be the network of relations that prevent collapse. While Damascus has been heavily damaged by the absence of electricity, the high cost of living and the bombings of homes, Aleppo has been hit even harder, with shortages of water, food and work. Nevertheless, families and individuals – at least, the majority of them – have not lost hope. There is a strong resistance that draws its real force from prayer, from solid faith and from definite hope, which are visible despite the hard blows that families receive every day with the death of children and young people, the emigration of young males and the steady loss of jobs.

What encourages me to go on in my daily mission despite the countless signs of death we witness every day is what Jesus said about the daughter of Jairus: "The child is not dead, but asleep" (Mk 5:39). There is still hope. In Aleppo, these words have become a parish priest's profession of faith, that of his parishioners and all Christians. This is the sentence that dwells in our hearts and on our lips; we say it untiringly, instead of the ancient professions of faith of the early Christians ("Jesus is the Lord" and "Maranatha", "Come, Lord Jesus")

The public mission of Jesus that continues in Syria today

In the past few days, the eucharistic liturgy has offered us Mark's account

5   The civil war in Lebanon lasted from 1975 to 1990. Over 100,000 people died.

of the public mission of Jesus. Jesus walked the streets of the city preaching the gospel, casting out demons and healing all sorts of illnesses. Thinking about my experience in Aleppo – in particular the difficult cases we deal with in the parish office – I find myself, as a believer and as a priest, continuing this public mission not only by healing the psychological and spiritual diseases of the body through the word of God and the sacraments, but also through small, daily, concrete gestures of charity. As Pope Francis said in his message for Lent, the church is the "hand of God", a hand that heals.[6] I also feel like part of this tender hand, that barely touches the deepest wounds of humanity and yet heals them. I am proud to be a part and an instrument of the tenderness of the Lord, a loving presence of the good shepherd. Every day, I feel that force of healing that is present in the word of God and in the sacraments, especially in the eucharist and in reconciliation. Lastly, I am increasingly aware of how this hand, an instrument of tenderness, has to be able to physically touch the leper before healing him.[7]

Visits in the Midan district

In Arabic, the name Midan means "the field". Since the chaos started in Aleppo, Midan has become a battlefield, in which it is easy to die. Many Christian families of Armenian origin live in this popular neighbourhood. The shops are next to the houses, built on top of one another. The houses are small and the buildings are tall, with five or six floors. This district has suffered and continues to suffer the worst fate. Families, the great majority of whom are very poor and with many children, cannot leave because they have nowhere else to go. So they stay in their houses,

....

6 "In the Incarnation, in the earthly life, death and resurrection of the Son of God, the gate between God and man, between heaven and earth, opens once for all. The Church is like the hand holding open this gate, thanks to her proclamation of God's word, her celebration of the sacraments and her witness of the faith which works through love." (From the Message of His Holiness Pope Francis for Lent 2015:)

7 "A man with leprosy came to him and begged him on his knees; 'If you are willing, you can make me clean.' Jesus was indignant. He reached out his hand and touched the man. 'I am willing,' he said. 'Be clean!' Immediately the leprosy left him and he was cleansed." (Mk 1:40-4)

only a hundred yards from the armed militia who continue to launch gas bombs, mortars and missiles. The noise of the shooting sounds unrelentingly. The streets are out of bounds, except if you run and risk your life; snipers aim at and kill unarmed men and women who simply had to go out in search of work or to buy something to eat.

Two families whose homes were bombed, and who nevertheless continue to live in their greatly damaged houses, asked me for help to repair them, at least partially. After detailed evaluation, I suggested making limited repairs so that they could continue to live decently, even though there was a real danger of being bombed again.

On the day I went to visit these families, the father of the first one stopped me a few steps before the building to explain where and how the gas bomb fell, destroying his balcony, the windows and doors. Staring at me, he said: "Father, it is an immense joy that you come to our home at this time of great danger and despite all your engagements. My wife and I are speechless with happiness for this visit; you are bringing us the blessing of the Lord."

At the entrance to the building, he showed me the road where 18 people were killed by an armed militia sniper who shot at innocent people. When I went in, I blessed the rooms with holy water, and we prayed in front of a small icon of the Virgin Mary, where the man usually prays with his wife. Because of the snipers, the man (who had learned the safest ways to go) was concerned for my safety and took me to the second house. He did not enter, out of respect for the intimacy of its inhabitants.

The second house belongs to a newly-wed couple. The husband worked as a driver but he has lost his job and is finding it hard to find something to do. His wife is a housewife. The apartment is made up of a bedroom, kitchen and a very small room where four people can sit closely packed together. It was this room that was hit while the couple were in the house. The explosion made a hole in the roof, destroying one wall and all the furniture, which, being very poor, was destroyed in the fire. Since then, the wife has suffered from nervous exhaustion but her husband, despite all his worries, has never lost his smile. After praying with them, I blessed them together with what little remained of the house and I examined the rebuilding that had already started.

There was a third case: a mother of five children who told me that her husband has been urgently taken to hospital because he suffered from viral cirrhosis of the liver. She is a housewife, the husband had not been working recently and the five children were too small to work. How could she pay the hospital, for the prescriptions and for the very expensive medicine needed to cure the disease? In the parish, we contacted the clinic where the man was admitted and promised to cover all the expenses of his stay and medicines. After he was discharged, the man went home tired and without strength. Now he needs another treatment and a lot of care, but to receive them he has to go to Homs or to Damascus.[8] One day, I found the whole family in a room, the children huddling like chicks around their mother and the father completely exhausted. They told me about how, in their experience, Providence never failed them. They told me of their hopes that the war would end soon and that the oldest daughter, who was in university, would finally be able to graduate and work in order to help the family. We prayed, then I blessed them, assuring them that the gentle hand of God, that is the church, will always be close to them.

Going back to the parish, as I was reflecting on the gift of these meetings, I realised that I had travelled down a real via crucis. I had entered deeply into the mystery of the suffering of Jesus, his death and his resurrection. As I went from one house to another in that area that had been hit so badly, it seemed to me that I was covering the stations on the via crucis in the Old City of Jerusalem with my brothers. I hope that the Lord gives me the strength never to stop experiencing that via crucis every day, so that I can be a sign of his love.

The gentle hand of God

Was it worth visiting the half-destroyed houses that men, women and children live in? Could I not have determined the necessary aid from afar, without exposing myself to the risk of a sudden encounter with death? These are questions which, as a parish priest, I continued to ask myself until Jesus himself gave me the answer through another question. Was it worth touching the leper before healing him? Wasn't it possible to heal him without touching him? If it is about showing the gentleness of the

8 Aleppo is about 185km from Homs and about 360km from Damascus.

27

Lord that cancels all the divisions between man and his God, the gesture of touching is the heart of what can be called the divine liturgy of healing.

Visiting houses in Midan is the best and truest way of witnessing to how even today Jesus is not ashamed of touching leprosy to show how present it is. There is nothing more concrete than the gentle touch of the church that helps to repair a home damaged by bombs or heal a father otherwise condemned by a serious disease. These deeds are worth much more than words because they have the strength to heal, even to resuscitate from death.

The act of touching the leper is related to another one which shows the immense gentleness of God; it is the compassionate gift of food Jesus gives to the starving crowds after multiplying the loaves and fishes (Mk 6:34-44). One spontaneously thinks of the words of the Acts of the Apostles: "It is more blessed to give than to receive!" (20:35)

15 JUNE 2015

We have recently started summer camp for children and teenagers. On the first day, there were 51 and now just a few days later there are already 120. We started these initiatives because we wanted to prevent the poor children who cannot leave Aleppo from having to spend the whole summer shut up at home. We want to give them the chance to play, meet and spend happy and peaceful times together; we want to help them grow up and socialise, so that they can cultivate all their talents.

Rejoice in the Lord always!

This is the motto of our summer camp: "Rejoice in the Lord always, I will say it again: Rejoice!" (Phil 4:4). These are the words of St Paul, who invites us to rejoice because Jesus himself is our joy.

At first, the parents were very frightened by the idea of letting their children leave home and they did not have the courage to come to us to enrol them. We phoned all the families to convince them. The day of the inauguration was an extraordinary day of festivities, with singing, dancing, sweets and even a clown. The mothers and fathers were amazed and moved, even more than the children.

We started the activities with children from the first to fifth years of primary school, aged from six to 10, but the smallest ones immediately started to protest, in tears, because they also wanted to join in. We listened to them as well and now we have 25 tots aged between three and six. Today, in all, we have 120 children and teenagers. Thanks to Providence and to the Spirit, the number of volunteers who help us is growing and, unexpectedly, many mothers have also become involved.

Often the internet here does not work, so children and parents with no access to virtual relations necessarily have to open up to the world of real relations. This makes them healthier from all points of view: human, psychological, intellectual and spiritual. Parents have asked us on several occasions to keep the summer camp open every day of the week, but we answered that it is fundamental for the children to have time to spend at home. We do not want to replace families. We want to cooperate with them to assist the human growth of the children.

The activities and programme of the summer camp

Though the summer camp is open four days a week from 9am to 1.30pm, at 8.30am people already knock on the door asking to come in. The camp is different every day and takes place in different spaces, depending on the activity. Children play and let off steam and are helped in their perception of reality and their intellectual growth. We arrange cooking lessons and the children take turns preparing lunch. We all eat together.

Their spiritual growth is particularly important to us and so every day we propose a moment of prayer, a song or a story, which are always different, about the life of Jesus. On Sundays, children liven up the Mass. Many of the youngest children are malnourished, so we try to give them milk, as well as chocolates and sweets to make them happy.

The National Sports Institute just offered us a facility with instructors and so every Saturday, or second Saturday, we go there by bus and the children play various sports like basketball, football or volleyball.

The church's embrace in everyday toil

The real and deepest reason for organising the summer camp is the desire for people to perceive the signs, even if small, of the delicacy of Christian charity, which can also show itself in the gift of a toy or a need taken that is care of. This way, suffering is purified and the eyes of those around us start to see. The heart starts to feel the presence of the divine in everyday life through the loving embrace of the church. We want to reinforce the perception of the face of Christ present, the tender face of God turned towards his suffering people.

PART III

In early July, the rebels launched a heavy attack against the western part of the city, which continued non-stop for five days. They succeeded in conquering strategic positions to the detriment of the regular army. This was the shower of 400 missiles that Father Ibrahim talks about.

6 JULY 2015

It is a miracle to have a few minutes of internet connection to be able to read and reply to some messages. The past few days have been very troubled. There is talk of 400 missiles and bombs dropped on our area, which is controlled by the regular army. There have been many deaths and injuries, many new stories of profound suffering.

In the parish, "like a weaned child with its mother" (Ps 131:2) we continue on our path of trusting abandonment in the hands of the Father, giving him everything that we are, our faithful and the people who are close to us. All the mystery is hidden in this gesture of trusting surrender, in abandonment to the hands of the Lord. We continue the projects that we have already started, with small but determined steps: the summer camp, meetings with engaged couples, wedding anniversary celebrations and visits to houses, to bless homes and pray with families.

Yesterday, despite the difficulties, after evening Mass I was able to visit two families and I returned to the monastery late in the evening full of joy and amazement for the faith that I saw working in our parishioners. On some days, we have no fewer than 150 children at our summer camp. We have new projects for them. Along with food, which we distribute continuously, we would like to give them underwear, trousers, t-shirts and shoes. We are happy about the things that we can do. It is all thanks to Providence, which helps us through our brothers and sisters in faith.

13 JULY 2015

At last, a great joy. The water is back today after being cut off for 11 days. People had been coming in desperation, hoping to get some water from the well in our monastery. Making enormous sacrifices, we pump the water from the well using a large electric generator which consumes diesel fuel in large quantities.

There has been practically no supply of electricity in Aleppo for some time. Its inhabitants buy electricity from private generators that have appeared along the streets, but these burn diesel fuel, polluting the air and making it unbreathable. The cost of enough electricity to light a small lamp in the evening is so great that many families have resigned themselves to staying in total darkness.

The people here are humiliated every day. Yesterday in my homily during Sunday Mass, I asked them to bear the cross with joy and with a smile and to thank God for the gift of the water that has returned, instead of complaining about the many days of its absence. We are walking up a long uphill path, but the Lord himself offers opportunities to sanctify us and increase all our virtues, especially those of patience and trusting abandonment.

PART IV

Life in Aleppo is absurd, as Father Ibrahim writes in this letter. Even in a relatively calm period, a missile can fall in the neighbourhood. Suddenly, everything changes.

29 SEPTEMBER 2015

The past three days have been rather hard. A missile fell just behind our church of St Francis in the district of Azizieh, a densely-populated and crowded area. It was afternoon and people were resting or strolling in the streets. The next day, I went to visit the homes damaged by the explosion and I saw an immense expanse of rubble and ruins. Fortunately, the damage is mostly to the buildings; there are only a few minor injuries. I perceived so much pain and sadness in hearts, as well as fear and despair. I prayed with families in their bombed homes. As soon as I returned to the monastery, I distributed aid for repairs. Immediately afterwards, I learnt of other atrocious bombings in various parts of Aleppo from different families who came to us friars in despair, asking for help. One father confided in me that he had already repaired his home twice after it was damaged by the bombs and that this third time he could not even imagine beginning the work again. He left with his wife and children, finding refuge with his parents-in-law, even though their apartment is very small.

Numerous families had their homes destroyed and there is no way to repair them. Their neighbourhoods have become a continuous target and it is inadvisable for the residents to go back there to live. The bombings are unfortunately increasing considerably, both during the day and at night. The population is suffering enormously. Many can no longer sleep for even an hour at night. Even so, the few lucky ones who still have a job go to work in the morning despite everything. Yesterday the water was cut off again, complicating the situation and beginning a new period of daily distribution of water to homes. We use trucks or plastic containers, giving precedence to the elderly.

Life in Aleppo is absurd and I no longer ask why people try to emigrate, why they take to the sea, risking everything, even their lives. According to human reason, staying here is madness. We friars stay regardless, to help the people. This is the time to be present, be close to people and look after the poor and all those who suffer. With them, we are poor. With them we suffer and pray to our Father, the provident and full of mercy.

12 OCTOBER 2015[9]

Syria is living through a tragedy in the present and is losing its future. This is particularly clear here in Aleppo, the city-martyr of this dirty war. There are no official figures for the whole of Syria, but in the past three months – the most difficult so far – about 10 per cent of my parishioners have left, in an unstoppable flow of emigration both to other cities in the country and outside Syria.

We are witnessing the emptying of the country, especially of its young men: engineers, doctors, school head-teachers and all teachers. Even in our parish, we are witnessing this continuous loss to all the parish groups and associations. Here is one example. In the past few months we have had to appoint new people in charge of the choir to replace those who have gradually left, ending up with people who are increasingly less experienced. Now we have to reckon with the lack of expert collaborators, people who for many years have been fundamental in the parish's activities.

This migration, which concerns many people and whole families, is spontaneous and chaotic. The people who flee are exposed to dangers that are no less serious than staying in Aleppo under the bombs, including the risk of death, as shown by the tragedies at sea or along the overland routes. Once safe, the family which has emigrated may

9   This article by Father Ibrahim was published in *Avvenire* on 12 October 2015 with the title, "A cry of pain from Aleppo, the city-martyr.".

experience an internal breakdown; the parents are unable to overcome the first, very difficult phase of adaptation and experience a real culture shock. The sudden change in living conditions often also has a severe psychological impact, resulting in the loss of inner peace and making people highly vulnerable.

We friars try to do the impossible to curb this haemorrhage, supporting individuals and families in various ways. However, we cannot force anyone to remain, nor, on the other hand, do we encourage anyone to leave. As the situation of total chaos and lack of security, electricity, water, diesel fuel, food and work continues, it is certainly not difficult to understand why so many decide to leave the country.

Europe has to listen to the frank and direct words of Pope Francis. On several occasions, he invited Europe to welcome refugees and emphasised the need to recognise the real reasons for this emigration and to try solve the dramatic problems at the root of it. This is fundamental because it implies a deep conversion of thought and action in order to change the way of doing politics. Unfortunately, several countries – if they listen at all – only listen to the first part of the Pope's appeal, shutting themselves up and completely ignoring the more difficult second part.

Our experience with refugees has taught us to say that charity is needed, but it must be true charity. Borders have to be opened and all these suffering people have to be looked after without distinction. However, it is also necessary never to stop discerning and evaluating; many of our Christian brothers who have moved to Europe have told us that, on their journey, they were close to people who were migrants like themselves but who had the "seeds" of the Islamic State inside them. They were so certain of impunity that they spoke of it in loud voices, without any scruples.

We will never tire of repeating that abandoning Syria or the Middle East to its fate would be a tragedy for the whole of humanity. Incalculable damage has already been done to the testimony of the historical presence of Christ, a terrible injury to the announcement of the gospel, which should never cease to echo in this land. The Lord has given no one permission to uproot the tree of Christianity which was grafted here and has grown here for 2,000 years, watered by the blood of martyrs and the testimony of countless saints. By "no one", I don't mean only not Islamic fundamentalists but not us, the 2,000-year-old church of the Orient, either.

With this surrender comes the certainty that God is present today in the rubble of Aleppo, that the "gates of Hades will not overcome it" (Mt 16:18) and that the Lord always causes more good to flow, even out of evil, for those who love him. We continue to encourage our people to hope against all hope, bearing the cross of every day with courage. As St John Chrysostom said in a letter written during his last exile, the black clouds and the storms that run through the whole history of the church already announce the fine weather that will come tomorrow. In our assiduous prayers, we find the energy to continue to see with the eyes of the heart that there is something beautiful and luminous which, after this storm, awaits the church of the Orient. We await, not in vain, a new time for testimony and the expansion of the Kingdom of God.

PART V

Father Ibrahim wrote this letter a few hours after jihadits groups – under threat of Russian airstrikes and the regular army advancing from the south – attacked his church. On 30 September 2015, the Russian raids had started, with almost 700 attacks in three weeks. For days, the whole region of Aleppo had been under the fire of the Russian raids and of the Iranian-Syrian offensive, with at least 70,000 civilians fleeing.

25 OCTOBER 2015

After various unsuccessful attempts to damage our Latin cathedral of St Francis, this afternoon during the 5pm Mass some jihadist groups were able to hit the dome. It happened as I was about to distribute communion. We have to thank the Lord because the dome withstood the strike, which exploded outside. The explosion did not enter the building. There were a few seconds of real panic, when the earth shook continuously and all around us we could only see dust, beams and pieces of plaster that were falling on top of us. Luckily, only seven people were slightly injured and one more seriously, now undergoing in-depth examination. We will not stop giving thanks to the Lord for having prevented fatalities.

The attempt to destroy the dome during the Sunday evening Mass, when the church was full of worshippers, was not by chance, nor was the fact that all of us are safe; we were protected by Mary, Mother of God and our mother. We hope that this chaos comes to an end and that we will soon be able to speak of these episodes as events in the past, without the fear that they may be repeated at any time.

On the days before that dramatic Sunday of 25 October, the bombings by the jihadists – who have absolutely no scruples about bombing the poor unarmed and peaceful civilians who live in the area controlled by the regular army – hit the neighbourhoods of Aleppo non-stop from various directions. The jihadist troops felt threatened by the advance from the south of the regular army supported by Russian air raids.

That Sunday then, the church of St Francis was hit and its dome, only by a miracle, did not collapse on the worshippers and cause a disaster. It is clear that the jihadists launched the gas canister from a launch base for missiles and that they chose the place and the time with great care, to cause the greatest damage possible to a Christian building. The objective, not by chance, was the dome, the most fragile part of the roof. The timing was also chosen with great accuracy: Sunday evening Mass. This Mass is the parish's main celebration, the most crowded one. They chose precisely the last part, when there is the distribution of communion. It was 5.45pm.

Interminable seconds

The gas canister hit the dome, only causing external damage as it did not explode. It rolled away and fell on the roof of clay tiles supported by large wooden beams and cement. The canister exploded there loudly.

At that moment, I was holding the Most Holy Sacrament and distributing communion to the faithful, who were standing in a line in the centre of the church. I only had time to give it to five or six people, then we heard a distant noise, not very loud, like something heavy that was falling on the roof. Not more than 10 seconds went by and the whole church began to shake for about 40 interminable seconds. A shower of stones, plaster and pieces of glass was pouring down on us and we could hardly see anything. Covered in dust, I heard my frightened sheep screaming in despair and hiding at the sides and in the corners of the church while the floor continued to shake.

Realising that some faithful had remained between the pews in the centre of the church screaming in pain, I took a few steps towards the altar to put down the Blessed Sacrament. Then I went back to help. I wanted to act as quickly as possible, because the jihadists usually launch a second missile at the same place immediately after the first. Fortunately this did not happen. There were no dead, but we soon discovered that more than 20 people sustained minor injuries.

The faithful, still terrified, did not know what to do. After having made sure that there were no fatalities, I beckoned to those who had stayed in the church to go out into the garden by the side doors; there I continued to distribute communion. We also recited an Our Father, an Ave Maria and the Gloria, as thanks to Jesus and to Mary. The celebration came to an end with the solemn blessing.

The blood-stained hosts, symbol of communion with the Lord

In the sacristy I realised that the hosts in the pyx were stained with the blood of some of the worshippers. This made a great impression on me, more than seeing the church covered in dust, plaster and broken glass. The hosts mixed with our blood were an unequivocal sign of the presence of the Lord in communion with us; it was as though they shone with the light of consolation and peace.

The participation of the faithful

In this drama, it was a deep consolation to meet various men, especially youngsters, who although they had not been present at the Mass came running to offer their help. I asked them to remove the rubble and clean the floor, preparing the church as best as possible for Mass the next day.

The following morning at 7.30am I had the large bells rung. They had not been used for some time due to the power cuts. The bells called the people to take part in Mass in the bombed church. Afterwards, we invited those attending into the lounge of the monastery for coffee. Together, we discussed what had happened, thanking the Lord once again for having saved us. The day continued and more than 30 women arrived, determined to clean everything up. The reaction of our faithful to such a terrible trauma was truly admirable.

The bombs are now falling continuously and everywhere. The danger of other attacks on our church is present, but this must not frighten us. I keep repeating to the Christians of my parish that they must not be afraid to come to church and attend Mass. We are blessed if we die close to the Lord, in his house, rather than alone and prey to fear in our homes.

On the morning of 25 October, the day of the bomb on the church, we held the catechism lesson for 166 children. On the following Sunday, 1 November, All Saints' Day, the catechist and I wondered whether the children would be brave enough to come. 160 came. What's more, the number of people who come to Mass increases day by day.

A strength that comes from the Father

Some parishioners have asked me how I was able to react so calmly and with a smile, without losing the peace of my heart and prudence. I answered that I felt a greater strength inside myself. It was the strength of the Lord who guided me and his advice that moved me. I could not have guided the events and decided to invite the frightened worshippers into the garden to receive communion, giving thanks with prayer. It was certainly not me, but God who was speaking and acting through me. Are not fortitude, counsel and wisdom three of the seven gifts of the Holy Spirit?

A song to the Lord who saved us

The evil planned against us was enormous. If the gas canister had made a hole in the dome and entered the church, there would have been dozens of dead. If the huge chandelier hanging from the dome had fallen, it would have killed everyone who was underneath it waiting to receive communion. The Lord, however, who allows evil out of respect for our freedom, scaled it down, directing it only towards the stones and saving all of us. He glorified himself through evil, giving us another sign of his love. As a consequence, instead of moans and screams of terror and fear, we raised a hymn of thanks to him, brimming over with love.

How an instrument of death becomes a symbol of peace and forgiveness

At the children's Mass on 1 November, a large fragment of the exploded gas canister found on the roof of the church was decorated, covered with flowers and transformed into one of the offerings to take to the altar. The symbol of hate and death was baptised, in a way, and became a sign of the love that forgives and gives life.

They send us death and we answer with life. They launch hatred at us and we offer love in exchange, through that charity which appears in forgiveness and though prayer for their conversion.

PART VI

Between October and December, the Syrian government and the Lebanese Shi'ite movement Hezbollah launched an offensive in the area south of Aleppo. This also contributed to keeping the city in the eye of the storm.

6 DECEMBER 2015[10]

Choosing the door of the Latin church of St Francis in Aleppo as the holy door for the Jubilee of Mercy is a decision that filled our hearts with joy and gratitude.[11] When it was taken, only a few days had passed since the launch of the gas canister on the church's dome.

Pope Francis never tires of repeating that church by nature is an open door, so that the sinner can feel the embrace of the Lord. It is a door from which the mercy of the Father offered to all gushes. Today is a time of grace, the time of the jubilee to celebrate the mystery of God's mercy, the return of the prodigal son, but also a time for conversion and spiritual renewal for the elder son (Lk 15:11-32). It is a time when the doors of the church are opened wide to everyone, not only to the faithful, but also to those who are in search of the mystery.

Since I arrived here a year ago as head of the Latin community I have understood my role in Aleppo, a city martyred by war, as a service of opening doors, more precisely of opening the door of the mercy of God to all those who are suffering and living together with us. This is possible only when one's heart is wounded by divine love, open

10 This article by Father Ibrahim appeared in the December 2015 issue of *La Porta Aperta*, the monthly supplement of *Avvenire*, with the title "The wounds of Aleppo, lights of hope".

11 Pope Francis officially announced the Extraordinary Jubilee of Mercy on 11 April 2015. The holy year dedicated to mercy started on 8 December 2015, the solemnity of the Immaculate Conception, and ended on 20 November 2016.

to all and willing to welcome, a heart that offers itself to forgiveness and exudes that love which, as Pope Francis says, *primereas* us, gives before being asked.[12] Our Catholic community of the Latin rite is the poorest Christian community in Aleppo. We do not own land which can support us. We do not even have a bank account which lets us cope with the urgent needs caused by the war. This is what I tell all the families in the parish over and over again: "In spite of this, we are rich with the mercy and the love of the Father who gives us the charity between us." In our church, we have made a very Franciscan pact. We have agreed never to accumulate anything, emptying our pockets of even that little that we collect, as Francis of Assisi showed us, to help those who suffer.

Despite our poverty, we were able to distribute more than 100 water tanks to many families in urgent need. We have been dealing with the situation of 450 Christian families who, because of the crisis of the war, are no longer in a position to meet their monthly mortgage repayments. The banks have started legal proceedings against the families, who now risk being evicted from their homes. We contacted various heads of the Christian communities in the city, warning them of the danger, and we are raising awareness among various charitable associations. Paying at least 25 per cent of the families' debt, and thereby postponing the risk of their being thrown out of their homes, means that we are becoming a vehicle for the mercy of the Father.

Recently we have been able to give many families (80 per cent of which live under the poverty line) a voucher for 200 litres of diesel fuel, just enough for heating for the winter. We are helping with expenses for school and university. There are also daily needs to be dealt with: food, clothes, electricity, medical examinations and medicines. All this is like a dream, but it is thanks to Providence that the dream comes true, day

12 Pope Francis explained this expression in a homily on 31 July 2013 in the Church of the Gesù in Rome, on the occasion of the feast day of St Ignatius: "I seek Jesus, I serve Jesus because he sought me first, because I was won over by him: and this is the heart of our experience. However he goes first, always. In Spanish there is very expressive word that explains it well: El nos 'primerea', he 'precedes' us. He is always first. When we arrive he is already there waiting for us."

after day. We are poor, but we are able to enrich others by throwing the doors of our heart open wide.

Jesus, nailed to the wood of the cross and mocked until the very last instant, did not let hatred prevail. Instead, he forgave his tormentors, showing his over-abundant mercy. So it is not so strange that the church of St Francis, hit and crucified by hatred and bearing the marks of devastation, opens a door so that the mercy of our Father can flow over those who decide to come through it. The door will be open for a whole year (though we hope it might always be open) to Christians desirous of renewing their life by becoming increasingly like Christ. It will also be open to all those who, although perhaps still living in hatred (like those who fired the bomb on us) are living through a crisis of their humanity and are in search of a way out from the hell that has entered their hearts.

We have transformed all the spaces of our monastery into an oasis of peace and love, where people can rest for however long they need and can meet God. Our community is a pure spring of healing and mercy, a source of the announcement of the newness of life brought by Christ.

12 December 2015

With the blessing of the Lord, today in our church of St Francis of Assisi, the holy door was opened for the Extraordinary Jubilee of Mercy. The Apostolic Vicar of the Latins Msgr Georges Abou Khazen celebrated. He was accompanied by bishops of various Oriental rites and many priests, who then took part in the Mass. The celebration started in the Maronite chapel and continued in a procession with songs and hymns of praise until the Latin church. After entering through the holy door the participants filled the church, colouring it with the liturgical shades of violet and white. During his homily, Msgr Georges explained the meaning of the jubilee.

Although Aleppo is living through very difficult moments due to the launches of missiles and bombs, the celebration brought great consolation to our hearts, as was apparent in the emotion in everyone's eyes, bishops and lay people alike. Our celebration is great and so is our joy, because ours is a merciful Father who gives his forgiveness to everyone.

23 December 2015[13]

All praise be Yours, my Lord, through Sister Water, so useful, so lowly, precious and pure.[14] It is precisely "Sister Water" that we miss so much here in Aleppo and that we wait for every day with hope and trepidation. We are in a permanent state of war and there are lots of nasty surprises at the start of our days: unprecedented waves of violence, bombs and shooting in the streets. All this always happens in inhabited areas. The scourge which currently afflicts us more than anything else is the unbearable water shortage, which is transforming this crisis into a real catastrophe. There are inhabited areas of Aleppo which have not received a drop of water for years. Even in neighbourhoods in which the water is on every now and again, the inhabitants live in a state of constant fear; water is cut off for days and sometimes whole weeks on end. Then it appears all of a sudden and, just as it came, it disappears again without any warning.

Apparently the state has started looking for alternative sources of supply, using underground water resources that in peace time it had strictly prohibited using in order not to accelerate the process of desertification. Now, though, the risk of desertification is secondary to the fact that people are dying of thirst.

People here are humiliated on a daily basis. It is impossible not to share the suffering and the sorrow of a father who can no longer provide for his small children or a man whose elderly parents are immobilised. Can you imagine those parents with serious back problems who, living on the fifth or sixth floor without a lift, have to carry the water the family needs to in order to survive on their shoulders all the way from the street to their door?

Heart-breaking moans are continuously coming from the streets; the cry of the innocents never stops. Our minds and hearts are constantly confronted with simple sentences like, "We have an elderly person dying at home" or "A neighbour of ours can no longer move, how can

---

13 This article by Father Ibrahim was published in *Avvenire* on 23 December 2015, with the title "Give us water, the cry from Aleppo".

14 Francis of Assisi, *Canticle of the Creatures*

she be helped?" Every time that the water is cut off for more than four days, all the phone calls we receive and all those who knock on the door of our office insistently plead for same thing: water.

From morning to night all the people of Aleppo rush to the public wells only sporadically made available to the population. In the streets, you never come across a man, woman or child walking without a bucket or a bottle, because drinking means survival. Unfortunately, there are no adequate sanitary controls on the wells and, as a consequence, there are cases of poisoning and intestinal infections. The various Christian communities of the different rites present in Aleppo do everything they can to help all those who are in need, but in no way can they replace the state or act as the Ministry of Water Resources. Some have begun to consider alternative temporary solutions, but perplexity and a sensation of impotence prevails. The scenario we are facing appears too challenging for our forces.

We Franciscan fathers are trying to live this tragedy with the imperative of mercy close to our hearts and help anyone who comes to us with their basic need for water. We bear in mind the words of the Lord: "I was thirsty and you gave me something to drink" (Mt 25:35). Every instant of our presence among the people of Aleppo can be read as the exercise of one of the 14 works of corporal and spiritual mercy.[15] This is how the Lord accompanies us, educating us to be merciful as our Father is merciful. For months, the doors of our monastery of Azizieh have been wide open and pipes transport water from the well in our garden to the pavement, so that everybody can come and fetch it as they need it. To make this service easier and to ensure that it takes place in an orderly manner, some men and young volunteers help the people waiting in line.

We also have five truck drivers and cars equipped with tanks and pumps that take water from our well to deliver it directly to the homes

15 "The works of mercy are charitable actions by which we come to the aid of our neighbour in his spiritual and bodily necessities. Instructing, advising, consoling, comforting are spiritual works of mercy, as are forgiving and bearing wrongs patiently. The corporal works of mercy consist especially in feeding the hungry, sheltering the homeless, clothing the naked, visiting the sick and imprisoned, and burying the dead" (*Catechism of the Catholic Church*, 2447)

of the families that are registered at our office. The working hours are from 7am until 8.30pm without a break. In the best conditions, up to 45 homes a day can be served but, from the fourth day of a water shortage onwards serving everyone becomes unrealistic; the list of families extends to 500 and increases every day. The Maronite church close to ours has three trucks that also take water from our well. In this way we try to inhibit the black market and the exploitation of this dramatic situation by the too many people who, like pirates, take advantage. We also give work to some fathers who would otherwise be unemployed.

With gratitude and tenderness I observe, contemplate actually, the young volunteers helping the elderly who come to fetch water and who find it hard to walk. The young people carry tanks of 10 litres in their hands and on their backs and go with the elderly to their homes. Every two days, these young Samaritans take 30 litres of drinking water to each elderly person assigned to them.

Our great fear is that our well will dry up. This danger is unfortunately real even though the well is 150m deep, because at the height of this crisis daily consumption of water can be up to 6,000l. So the risk is very real. On the other hand, in good conscience we cannot but answer the thousands of people who knock on our door begging for water.

The Franciscan monastery in Er-Ram also distributes water through pipes and taps. Electricity is cut off everywhere and therefore like us in Azizieh they also consume a lot of diesel fuel to make the electric generator work. The water of Er-Ram, unlike ours, is not fit for drinking, but can nevertheless be used for all other purposes, so it is useful for many who live nearby and who have no alternative.

The third Franciscan site in Aleppo is the College of the Holy Land,[16] where there is also a well, which unfortunately is not used for the general population. To make its drinking water available, a new electric generator would have to be purchased with all the accessories. We know that many buildings in the city do not have a tank to collect and keep drinking water, or the one that they had was damaged by the bombs. For this reason, in August we began to purchase

16 Despite its name, before the war the College of the Holy Land was not a school but a recreational centre and home for vocations.

tanks to distribute free of charge and we continue to give them out. To date, we have already given 180, but hundreds of other families have asked us for one and they are anxiously awaiting their turn. When a new tank is installed in a house (with no cost to the family) it is a marvellous gift from heaven. Having a tank full of water allows a family to continue its life in conditions that are almost normal for a little while after running water is cut off.

O Lord, how many burdens weigh on our weak shoulders, on us who are called to help and accompany the people who live in Aleppo! How many crosses weigh on the shoulders of the Syrian people! This Biblical scourge of drought is more than can be borne. Paradoxically though, in the penury of having only what is essential for life we are able to see the immense gift of grace that the Lord offers Aleppo: an extraordinary reserve of human resources and the beauty, truth and goodness of our communion. Also, in begging for water every instant we have rediscovered the importance of this simple and humble gift from the Lord. Today, you cannot drink a single glass of water in Aleppo without exulting and exclaiming with all your heart: all praise be yours, my Lord, through Sister Water, so useful, so lowly, precious and pure.

24 DECEMBER 2015

Christmas Eve

Yesterday and the day before yesterday we celebrated the rite of penitence as a community. The celebration was attended by hundreds of the faithful, who then availed of the sacrament of reconciliation. This morning, we went to visit the ill in the Saint Louis Hospital of the Sisters of St Joseph of the Apparition.

This evening, 24 December, we celebrated the Mass in the middle of the falling bombs. Seven missiles were launched against our area of Azizieh just 10 minutes before Christmas Mass began. The church was still crowded. We were very worried about the lives of those present, but luckily everything went well. Together we remembered all our dead.

At the end of the Mass, there was a procession with more than 80 children and youngsters, each holding a lit candle, to take the Child Jesus to the grotto of the nativity scene. We then met in the parish hall to exchange Christmas greetings. Going into the hall, the youngsters were given a bag full of chocolates and delicious biscuits. We ate some desserts and listened to a choir of scouts who entertained us with Christmas carols. There was even a corner for children to take photos with Father Christmas. Everyone was very happy.

We asked the child Jesus for the gift of joy and peace, the opposite of the feelings that dominate in the hearts of many here in Aleppo, i.e. sadness, worry and fear. At the end of the small party, we friars dined together with joy and gratitude.

Comfort in difficulty

Here in Aleppo we are still living through very difficult times. The bombings are continuing and as a result the number of injuries, deaths and destroyed homes is increasing. There has been no electricity for 45 days. For three days, yet again, no water has come out of the taps and we cannot say when it will return. It is precisely in these dramatic, complicated and painful situations that we most feel the presence of our Father. He appears faithfully in the human face of Jesus, "Who, being in very nature God, did not consider equality with God something to be used to his own advantage; rather, he made himself nothing by taking the very nature of a servant being made in human likeness. And being found in appearance as a man, he humbled himself by becoming obedient to death – even death on a cross" (Phil 2:6-8). This is how the Lord became flesh for us, docilely taking our sufferings and our sin on himself.

In this scenario of total confusion for Syria and for each of us, he allows us to experience peace as a gift that comes from heaven, instant by instant, day by day. We are increasingly convinced that this gift has to be received with effort so that we can be made fertile in our hopeful waiting for a new time of grace.

When Mary was tired before the birth, Joseph was always at her side. When Mary was weak after the birth of the child, together with Joseph, Jesus was there to console her and sustain her. In the difficulties we are facing, all of you are alongside us and we feel you close like the limbs of the single mystical body of our Lord; you are our comfort and support.

Merry Christmas to each one of you and happy new year.

PART VII

A massive offensive by the regular army started in early February. The inhabitants of the neighbourhoods already under government control hoped that it would be the decisive battle to free the city from the rebels. This is not what happened. The army's initiative provoked a reaction from the jihadists, who heavily bombed the Christian neighbourhoods as well.

7 FEBRUARY 2016

Bombings in the Sulaymanieh-Ram area

I will try to relate what we have been going through in Aleppo since the offensive of the regular army has started to regain possession of the city.

On the night between three and 4 February, two missiles launched by the jihadists hit the area of Sulaymanieh-Ram, where our annexe is. Just when we received news of what had happened, I had been thinking about bringing all the friars of Aleppo together in a local pastoral chapter to decide together how we could intensify the service provided in Sulaymanieh and Midan.

The result of incessant bombing is always the same: death and destruction, the death of innocent citizens and the destruction of their poor houses. two Christians were killed, there were many injuries and countless houses were damaged. How can we not be disheartened? We had just finished repairing, though roughly, the damage caused by the missiles that fell on 12 April 2015, when these new bombs came, destroying what had been rebuilt with immense effort and many sacrifices.

Until then, our church had not been damaged in any significant way. The roof of the catechism classrooms, however, was partially destroyed, the walls were also damaged by the vibrations caused by the explosions and the windows were shattered. A missile hit our annexe, making a hole in the roof. It destroyed the statue of the Virgin Mary. The statue smashed into a thousand pieces and our sorrow can easily be imagined. A second missile fell in the street, damaging the entrance to the annexe and killing two Christians. The nearby buildings, like several times in the past, were not spared.

We friars immediately went to visit the families in the houses around the Er-Ram branch of the parish. We listened to the suffering and the grief of the mothers and fathers in the homes of the two men who lost their lives. They told us what happened in detail, allowing us to share their fear and inhabit their suffering. We are trying to be close to our people in every possible way as they knock continually on our door seeking help and comfort.

The Er-Ram branch of the parish attracts families from Sulaymanieh and Midan to Mass. The latter asked us for shelter after the church of Bisharat (Annunciation) in Midan was destroyed. Because the Maronite churches in the neighbourhoods have either been razed to the ground or are unfit for use we have also hosted the Maronite Christian community, which celebrates a number of Masses in our church during the week. Various parish groups meet in our house for their gatherings and a school for the deaf and dumb also receives hospitality. It is one of the very few centres of this type that is still active in Aleppo today. In addition to hospitality and the spiritual services mentioned, we share with anyone who comes to our door the most precious asset in Aleppo: the water from the wells in the annexe and the monastery.

The Christian neighbourhood of Midan

Strikes by jihadist groups and rebels responding to the advance of the government forces and their allies continued during the night between 4 and 5 February. Once again, we were hit in the heart. The explosions hit the mostly Christian neighbourhood of Midan. The destruction was devastating; the few inhabitants left are homeless once again.

Try to imagine what it means for us to be here while missiles and bombs fall unceasingly, even at night. We don't know what will happen to our parishioners in any moment, to our friends or their home, the place of their family story and deepest emotions. We don't know whether they, their children or the elderly will survive.

An elderly woman was crying, saying that people did not know what to do: leave their homes, run away and risk death on the road or stay shut up inside their homes, with the equally real risk of being destroyed by missiles. Some families decided to spend the night in the cold at the entrance to their homes, others under the stairs.

A lady who was holding her child knocked on our door asking for help and telling us that many people were buried under the rubble. Her screams had been of no avail. Nobody had come to help, nobody had the courage to answer. The injured remained buried for hours, alongside the corpses.

Welcoming, listening and acting

But we will not give up. During our visits to the damaged homes, accompanied by an engineer to evaluate the damage and the possible emergency repairs, we distributed tins of basic staple foods. Work began immediately on repairing doors and windows. Those whose homes had been irreparably damaged were helped economically to rent another one for three months, with the possibility of extension. Very many people, especially families with small children, come to us terrified. Most of them cannot even think of fleeing. A lot of money is needed for the journey and these families do not even have enough money for food.

In such a tragic situation, all that remains for us to do is welcome them and listen to them. After that, we have to act quickly; putting anything off until tomorrow is not an option. The work is immense and the needs are enormous.

The problems of water and prohibitive prices

The problem of drinking water remains, but people also need water for personal hygiene. People are so desperate that they go around under the rain of missiles hoping to get water from the taps installed in the streets, near wells. No water has come out of the taps for 10 days now.

Today the value of the dollar rose to 410 Syrian pounds, while only yesterday it was at 400. The prices of staple foods like bread, vegetables and so on are constantly going up. One woman who still has a job, and therefore a monthly income, explained to us that she could no longer afford even one dish of vegetables a day.

"How long, O Lord, will you forget me?"

In the grief of these days, the verse "How long, O Lord, will you forget me? How long will you hide your face from me?" (Ps 13:2) often comes to mind.

The questions that we would never like to hear at times rise spontaneously in us and in the small flock that still remains in Aleppo. Where is the Lord? Perhaps he has abandoned us? Faith is shaken at the root.

On the road to Damascus the Lord asked Saul, "Why do you persecute me?" (Acts 9:4), leaving us a confirmation of his communion with all the limbs of his mystical body the church. We too, Christians persecuted and the church that resists in Aleppo, are part of this body. Christ becomes close. Suffering on the cross, he looks down at his people who are suffering too. He is present in the midst of his people, he helps them and assists them through the tender mercy of his shepherds. The enormous strain that we shepherds feel in the face of the ordeals to which our flock is submitted is not an obstacle or a scandal for us. It is this way for us Franciscan friars; it is the reason we decide to stay here day after day.

PART VIII

The rumour of a truce spread among the people of Aleppo in February. But this hope was immediately revealed as unfounded; the bombings continued, with all their tragic consequences.

10 MARCH 2016

The conditions of our families in Aleppo is, without a doubt, worse than those of the families who live in the other towns and cities of Syria. According to the latest survey, every family in Aleppo needs a minimum of 17,000 Syrian pounds (the equivalent today of about 35 euro) to obtain essential goods such as electricity, water and gas. According to our data, only five of the 600 families in our Latin community are still well-off; all the others live well below the poverty line. Indeed, even those families who had been rich in the past, have become impoverished and urgently need help after these five years of war. We see people who used to own prosperous industrial companies, with incomes that were in excess of hundreds of thousands of dollars, reduced to abject poverty. Having lost their workshops with all their machinery, they have remained alone with their bank debts, which they can no longer pay off.

Our statistics reveal that of our 600 families more than 250 are in abject poverty and with an income of less than 25,000 Syrian pounds a month (about 50 euro) they can no longer afford enough food to live decently. Recently, about 15 of our parishioners were admitted to hospital in need of blood transfusions to avoid death by malnutrition.

Two amps per family

The electricity shortage is one of our most serious problems. Electricity can only reach homes through local generators owned by private firms charging very high prices per amp. On average, families or people living alone need two amps to switch on two or three lights and the television or a radio. These two amps are not enough to run a washing machine or even the pump which, when water arrives, supplies the taps in the house. Two amps are therefore the minimum consumption for life not to go on in complete darkness, which we have seen can cause severe psychological disorders, leading to despair. A family with children in school or university cannot live without electricity. This is why we want to help those in abject poverty. They deserve to live with dignity. The project we call "two amps per family" is an important psychological support and an expression of solidarity.[17] Although there is talk of a ceasefire, yesterday and the day before bombing continued in a number of government-controlled areas, where almost all the Christians live. The situation in the city is still very critical and the electricity shortage is expected to last for up to one year. Our project aims to cover the cost of two amps per family per month for a year and therefore lets parents use the little money they still have to meet other basic needs.

25 MARCH 2016

Good Friday

I remember you in a special way in these days when the experience of the passion, death and resurrection of Jesus becomes more intense. Through purification by suffering, we reach the light of the salvific union with the Lord in Easter. It is this experience that has touched the life of all his apostles, a life otherwise marked by bitterness. But precisely for this reason his apostles are reinforced in faithfulness, in perseverance and in resolve to follow Jesus on that path which leads to the unconditional surrender of the self to the will of the Father, for the salvation of the world.

My wish, which becomes an intense prayer, is that our thinking and acting as humans should be perfect, so that our resurrection in Christ may also be perfect. May we keep nothing to ourselves, but offer

17 This year-long fundraising project was a collaboration with ACS (Aiuto alla Chiesa che Soffre/Aid for the Suffering Church.)

everything in sacrifice for love of the Lord. May everything we have be rendered as praise to the Lord.

Happy Easter.

11 APRIL 2016

The bombings have started again. two days ago, a missile fell in our area of Azizieh, destroying a house and damaging others. Last night, in some neighbourhoods such as Midan the situation was critical. Today the men who work in our monastery came with glistening and tired eyes after a sleepless night.

Inflation continues as people are finding it harder and harder to be able to earn anything to feed themselves and their dear ones.

Ours is a never-ending race. Although we have a good organisation and many volunteers and staff, the burden of humanitarian work is increasingly on us alone. Every day, more and more people knock on the door of the monastery. But there are also more and more families who thank the Lord for the presence of the friars who stay here in Aleppo to help the exhausted population.

PART IX

Father Ibrahim's community was struck in its heart: four missiles fell in the neighbourhood of Er-Ram, where there is a branch of the parish. One fell 20 yards from the church while Mass was being celebrated. The damage to the monastery and the college was enormous.

1 MAY 2016

What has been happening in the past few days in Aleppo is dramatic. We are living through the saddest and most painful days since the start of the war.

Today, during vespers, missiles fell all over the city, many in the areas of Azizieh and Er-Ram. In Azizieh, with the church packed for the start of the Marian month, we were nevertheless able to continue the celebration until the end. In Er-Ram, there were more than 70 people, including lots of children, at the 6pm Mass. Despite the bombings they continued the celebration until the very end. However, the priest was not able to give the blessing for the start of the Marian month because they all had to seek shelter quickly in the basement. Suddenly, they heard the noise of an explosion on the roof of the church and immediately afterwards the smell of burnt diesel fuel started spreading. For a few hours, they stayed in the basement trying to decide what to do. Then they decided to leave and go home.

We will have to wait until tomorrow to check the damage to our Er-Ram branch. In the area of Sulaymanieh alone, 13 missiles fell on the streets and the houses.

Many people who until now have been able to resist and did not want to leave are now starting to think of emigrating. Many are also prey to panic attacks and nervous breakdowns.

There is no end to the bombings. With every hour that passes, there are more deaths, injuries and houses destroyed. The part of the city under the control of the government forces, about a quarter of Aleppo, is deserted.

Yesterday, our church was packed for the Mass of the start of the Marian month. In contrast, during today's Mass almost half of the church was empty. People were not able to attend as usual because their house had been destroyed or because they had to go to the funeral of a relative.

Our cook called me to tell me that a missile had hit her house; it was only by miracle that there was nobody home at the time. She and her relatives were trying to retrieve her clothes and pieces of furniture that were not destroyed.

Our two cleaners were able to come to work today, but they were visibly upset. They have not slept for days. They have witnessed dramatic scenes of buildings collapsing around their homes and one of them had a missile fall on her home. In her case, it was a miracle that all the family survived. I told her to go home straight away to stay with her family and to rest.

Today, we also received the news of the death of two of our parishioners: a child and an 18-year-old. The child was 11 and had gone to his grandmother's to wish her a happy Easter. These are difficult days and it is difficult to smile.

People are fleeing and seek refuge with family or friends in safer parts of Aleppo. There are also long queues of people fleeing to seek refuge on the coast, near Latakia, a city controlled by the army and safer (although there the costs for survival are much higher than in Aleppo).

After the bombings that hit families, hospitals and innocent people, rebuilding starts immediately. We give concrete charity to those who have lost everything.

The Latin parish assumes the weighty commitment of repairing homes. For many, the church thus becomes an increasingly real family.

3 MAY 2016

This afternoon the Dabbit Hospital in the Muhafaza district was hit by a missile launched by the jihadists. 17 children died immediately, as well as men and women. Today, the state university was also bombed again and the government has announced the closure of schools. The bombings on our district have also intensified. Bombs are falling everywhere. The dead are being counted by the dozen and the wounded by the hundred.

There are no classes at school and the streets are as empty as when there was a curfew. The activities in the churches and parish centres are also reduced to a minimum. Many of our parishioners are suffering from panic attacks or nervous breakdowns.

What we are experiencing at the moment is an example of the cruelty of the jihadist militia, who have not accepted the truce and the path of dialogue and who continue to sow terror by launching missiles on crowded homes. In all the neighbourhoods, the houses with the poorest families have the largest number of occupants.

Six houses partly destroyed; tragedy and hope

In the Sulaymanieh-Hajj Habib area, six houses have been almost completely destroyed, with several others seriously damaged. We friars went there immediately, offering help. Our specialised group began repairs the day after the bombing. In this case, fortunately, none of the inhabitants (all Christians) were injured, nor were there any fatalities. There was, however, a lot of terror people's eyes, especially those of children.

In the tragedy, though, a small hope was kindled. Two families were moved to open their homes to neighbouring families in need. Another positive element is that, thanks to this emergency, we were able to meet other charitable associations that came to check the damage. The greatest challenge for us remains the repairing of the six houses that were partly destroyed. We estimate that it will cost 10,000 dollars to reinforce the foundations and rebuild the structure, 15,000 dollars for the woodwork, painting, buying new furniture or repairing it, and buying new clothes and toys. The risk is considerable because repairs have to start from the foundations, with the danger of compromising the walls.

The emblematic case of one family

The case of a Latin Catholic family from one of the bombed buildings is emblematic of many others: a mother-in-law living with her daughter-in-law and two sons. Both of their husbands have emigrated to Germany to try and help their families from there. The women have no other relatives in Aleppo. There is nobody to take care of them apart from the church, which is helping them every month through various projects.

When a missile fell on the building, the smallest child was sleeping and was covered by countless tiny stones and fragments of glass. By miracle, he continued to sleep and did not wake up until all the rubble was cleaned off him. The other child was in a state of shock for a long time. When we went to see him, he was looking for a toy and pair of trousers in the rubble on the balcony.

The Lord continues to perform real miracles, making his kindness and care tangible partly through us, not only through our commitment to repair homes, but also, in the case of children, through the provision of clothes and toys. For them, these small things are as fundamental as having a house and the miracle of Providence can be performed even through the gift of the objects of which they are fondest.

The church becomes family and home

Countless buildings have been reduced to rubble, as in Sulaymanieh-Hajj Habib. There are now families who no longer have a home, who no longer have anything. The church is everything for them. It is their family, their real home, therefore the first thing it must do for them is put a roof over their heads.

It has been calculated that from 23 April until today there have been 89 deaths and more than 500 civilian injuries in the areas under the control of the regular army.

MAPS

Syria political map showing the capital Damascus, national borders, other important cities, rivers and lakes (Peter Hermes/Shutterstock)

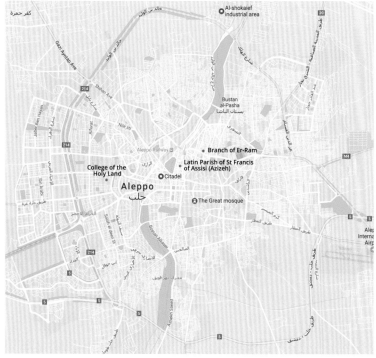

Source: Google Maps

The city of Aleppo covers a very large territory, comparable in size and its circular plan to that of Milan in Italy. Here, for the sake of simplification, we only show the city centre, indicating some important landmarks: the citadel, the great mosque and the railway station (places known to tourists and travellers), but in particular the Latin parish of St Francis of Assisi, the branch of Er-Ram and the College of the Holy Land, to which Father Ibrahim continually refers in these pages.

During the war, the government has always maintained control of the western part of the city (where the three Franciscan sites are), while the rebels settled in the eastern part. The line of the front (which we have not shown due to its continuous mobility) has, however, passed just a few blocks east of the parish of St Francis and the branch of Er-Ram. This explains the bombings and the destruction described in the book.

PHOTOS

"The explosions concerned the area of Midan, which is an area with a Christian majority." (p.54)

A group photo in front of the crib, with the children from the catechism class, January 2016

"Never would I have thought that I would have distributed a monthly food parcel," writes Father Ibrahim (p.145), but every month he prepares hundreds with his young volunteers for the poor of the parish.

The friars check the damage caused to Er-Ram by the bombings of early May 2016

The centre for the distribution of water in Azizieh: "We offered the water from our well" (p.158)

In February 2016, a missile hit the Er-Ram branch of the parish, making a hole in its roof and destroying the statue of the Virgin Mary. "It is easy to imagine our grief: the face of the Virgin Mary shattered to pieces in the middle of the street." (p.54)

"In the area of Sulaymanieh-Hajj Habib, several homes were seriously damaged. We friars intervened immediately (...) The day after the bombing the repair works started." Above, one of the bombed houses before the work (p.63)

Destruction in the area of Sulaymanieh-Hajj Habib

Celebration of Palm Sunday with the Bishop, Msgr Georges Abou Khazen at the church of St Francis in Azizieh

Distribution of food on Mother's Day in March 2016

The party at the end of the winter catechism classes 2016

"On some days at the summer camp, we have 150 children" (p.31). In 2016, there were 350 children!

A moment of tranquillity on the feast-day of St Barbara, 4 December 2015

Procession with the statue of the Virgin Mary at the end of the Marian month 2016

The Latin parish packed with the faithful for Mass ending the Marian month

Resuming work gives hope. The Latin parish, when possible, encourages small entrepreneurial projects.

"We can rent a shop for a year and see what we can do, maybe even with your help."
(p.159)

Father Firas Lutfi, brother of Father Ibrahim, playing with the children

"Recently we have started a course for engaged couples. We hope that more and more young people wish to get married, even in the tragedy of this senseless war." (p.123)

Father Ibrahim with some young people from the parish

A meeting with the group of women of the association of St Anthony of Padua at the College of the Holy Land, the third Franciscan site in Aleppo

"In the city, many buildings do not have a tank to collect and store drinking water [...] This is why, in August, we started to buy tanks to distribute free of charge." (p.48)

Father Ibrahim with the volunteers distributing water to the houses

Saying the rosary with the children from the catechism classes in the courtyard of the College of the Holy Land in January 2016

Meeting with the group of students and with their families

A visit to the outskirts of Gibrin and Hanano, where many refugees from the eastern part of Aleppo are camping, in January 2017

Destruction in the monastery of St Vartan, in the Midan area (January 2017): the war has really not spared anyone

6 May 2016[18]

I have only these few words with which to thank you, your parents and catechists for the charity that you are showing the children of Aleppo, who are in a condition of great suffering. The war in Syria has dragged the majority of the population into a state of prostration, in need of everything. But this evil, which we bear with patience and strength, has facilitated the revelation of your nature as real heroes of charity. Your small hearts have turned out to be much larger hearts, capable of welcoming, with love, lots of children like you, children who need your help and who even live on another continent.

Children of your age in Aleppo have asked me to thank you, ensuring each of you of their love and gratitude.

Charity will always be the first and last word above everything else. This is why we have to help each other and grow in charity, so that our life will increasingly be a demonstration of humanity and grace.

I am always praying for you, that you may grow up in age, wisdom and grace before God and men.

18 Letter to the children at an Italian Sunday school twinned with Father Ibrahim's through an initiative by ATS pro Terra Sancta

PART X

The fighting continued, especially south of the city, despite truce called for by Russia and the United States on 5 May. The regular army and pro-government militia, supported by the Russian Air Force, counter-attacked in the face of the rebel advance.

8 MAY 2016

Today there were numerous bombings again. A few minutes ago, two bombs fell in our area and a building collapsed in the district of Midan. People are still under the rubble; we do not yet know the number of dead and injured.

The families of the 18-year-old and 11-year-old killed by a missile were at the parish Mass this evening. The missile hit the child's grandmother's house while 15 people were there for Orthodox Easter celebrations. We prayed for these two martyrs and their families. Everyone was greatly moved and the church was full. During the homily, I spoke of faith, hope and charity as the roots of the Christian joy Luke speaks of in his gospel in the passage of the ascension.[19] I insisted on the charity the whole church shows us and on the charity that unites the Christians of Aleppo. I spoke about how it is the source of joy and consolation in

19 "He told them, 'This is what is written: the Messiah will suffer and rise from the dead on the third day, and repentance for the forgiveness of sins will be preached in his name to all nations, beginning at Jerusalem. You are witnesses of these things. I am going to send you what my Father has promised; but stay in the city until you have been clothed with power from on high'. When he had led them out to the vicinity of Bethany, he lifted up his hands and blessed them. While he was blessing them, he left them and was taken up into heaven. Then they worshipped him and returned to Jerusalem with great joy. And they stayed continually at the temple, praising God." (Lk 24:46-53)

the difficult times we are facing. After the blessing with the icon of the Virgin Mary, all the faithful greeted the families of the two boys with the words "Christ is risen!"

Everyone went home speaking about Christian charity, which leads us to a profound communion. The real miracle is the conversion of hearts – and what the Lord does in hearts here is more than a miracle.

8 MAY 2016[20]

For some time now we have noticed the warning signs of a new and frightening problem, on top of the countless ones we already have. Some banks, in difficulty after five years of war, have started to review their list of debtors: the long list of families who, having received loans, mortgaged their homes as guarantees. There is no peace for them. We have tried to find out the number of families involved and how many of them are Christians. Unfortunately the list was very long, containing hundreds and hundreds of families of whom 450 are Christian.

Quite a few months ago, a Syrian-Orthodox family knocked on the door of our monastery. They were terrified, with eyes that spoke of a great sadness and they did not conceal their fear. The father was the only source of income, with a monthly salary of 20,000 Syrian pounds which, at today's exchange rate, is less than 30 euro. They told us, agitatedly, of a large debt that had accumulated with the bank during these long years of war during which they had not been able to keep up with the monthly repayments. The bank went to court, which ordered them to pay or their house would be put up for auction. I answered that the jubilee had always been a particular time of grace and that it was possible to regain lost property and personal freedom. The Lord would not allow their family home to be lost and would not allow them to have to live in the streets; such a thing could not happen in this jubilee year. Therefore, I told them, in a few months the debt would be paid.

As I was speaking to that family, the beautiful story of a patriarch of

20 This article by Father Ibrahim was published in *La Porta Aperta*, a supplement of the newspaper *Avvenire*, with the title: "The fraternal hand that relieves Syrians from the burden of debts."

Alexandria, John the Merciful, came into my mind.[21] To help the poor, he ended up selling the lamps and all the furnishings in the patriarchal curia. After a few years, another poor man came knocking on his door, but he no longer had anything he could sell to help the man. John made him wait while he went to the market and sold himself as a slave and collected a few pennies. Luckily, as John was about to be put on show to be sold, a rich Christian happened to pass. Recognising his patriarch, he paid the price asked for him and restored him to freedom.

Influenced by the story of the holy patriarch and the endless flow of families who have continued to knock on the monastery door, I always answer them with a smile: "We have a lot of carpets and many furnishings in the monastery that we can sell before we will have to sell ourselves too."

200 families have already passed through our parish office. In order to effectively face this new emergency, we have set up a work group that includes a lawyer. In the first few months of 2016, with payments of an average of 900 euro per family, 115 families were relieved of the debts they had accumulated. The blessing and the consensus of their shepherds from the other rites, who warmly praised this courageous act, have been a great comfort for us. But the possibility of losing their home currently looms threateningly over the heads of hundreds of other Christian families. As there is no work in Aleppo, there is no income for the families, so almost all the women have already sold the little gold they had to meet the basic everyday food needs.

A young husband and father of a beautiful little girl, whose family benefited from our help, thanked me with tears in his eyes, confiding in me that the action of the church had given him a "new life". Both for him and for his family, seeing all the accumulated debts paid off was like the experience of the liberated people of Israel crossing the Red Sea. This is the way we were able to let so many families in Aleppo see, and perhaps experience as well, the force of the resurrection. We met in the lounge of the monastery to pray together with the first group of

21 A saint born in Cyprus who became famous for his charity. He became patriarch of the church of Alexandria in about 610. He called the poor his "lords". He died in 619 in Amatunte on the island of Cyprus.

families we helped, glorifying him who won and who continues to win our freedom from sin and death in everyday reality.

One father, who could not yet understand that the gift was free, asked me how he would be able to repay what he had received. I explained to him that he had only experienced a sample of Christian charity, which is without limits and without conditions, as it is in the image of what Christ offered for us on the cross: his very life. "If you want to repay somehow," I answered, "make sure that the flame of the charity that reached you is always burning in your heart, appearing both as thanks to the Lord and as a concrete action for your neighbour, especially the one who lives under the same roof as you."

PART XI

Father Ibrahim tries to come to Europe whenever he can, where he can count on the support of many. In 2016, he had various opportunities to take his testimony around Italy. Although the situation in Aleppo is increasingly critical and mourning is a daily occurrence, Jesus' heart does not close to the suffering of others. Father Ibrahim found words of comfort even for the earthquake survivors in central Italy.

7 SEPTEMBER 2016

On 16 June I was in Rome. Divine Providence guided my steps to the church of Saint Philip Neri, where I stood in great admiration before his icon and his relics. In those moments I remembered you, one by one, and I entrusted you, your parents and families to the Lord, through the intercession of this great saint. In front of the icon of the saint, I thought of how his life had been totally given to the Lord and to his smaller and needier brothers, the children left alone in the streets. He came from far away; Divine Providence guided his steps to the gates of Rome, to the church where he then spent his whole life. The Lord asked him to stop there, speaking to his heart through the children who looked at him and through their needs. His life was thus one of giving without limits and without conditions to children in need of accompaniment, in need of education, in need of being directed towards the discipleship of Christ. He did not shrink from this but plucked up courage, carrying out the mission which had been revealed to him and opening up a new path for the whole Church with the creation of the oratories.

There is a saying in Arabic: "A child does not grow up without a lion dying." It refers to the human and spiritual accompaniment parents give their children. It makes us understand how difficult it is to accompany children growing up and how many sacrifices educators have to make for children to grow up: the lion, a symbol of strength, has to give his life for a child to be able to grow up. This expression explains everything that our mission entails. As in the time of St Philip Neri, we are living in an age in which there are socio-political and cultural problems that are bigger than us. Many times we are unable to solve them and we go through them with our people. They are real challenges to our service as educators and helpers. Our answer is Jesus, supported by the Holy Spirit, an answer that has the power to change the future of society, families and people. Our only way is generously giving to our brothers.

Today there are many ways to educate and accompany children: parents, school, friends, television, the internet, etc. There are many challenges to a human and spiritual education becoming a path alongside Jesus. We have to trust that our education is the most powerful. The more we become part of the life of Jesus, the more the Spirit of Jesus gives testimony through our word, which becomes his word, which creates, purifies and heals, illuminates and unites people.

Please keep praying for us; we need every type of help. May the Lord give us the strength not to keep anything for ourselves, but to give ourselves completely for our brothers.

14 SEPTEMBER 2016

With great sadness we have heard the news of the earthquake in Italy. We immediately offered holy Masses and prayers for the souls of the dead, the injured and the families and friends of the people affected. In Aleppo, we live as though there is a continuous earthquake that shows no signs of ending. Our via crucis has been going on for more than five years, together with the slow death of the Syrian people. This part of the mystical body of Christ is increasingly short of breath: its strength is diminishing, the body is consumed by flagellation and blows. This past month has been atrocious in terms of the bombs and missiles that fall without respite. In our visits to homes, we notice increasingly heavy damage, caused by weapons that are more and more destructive.

I will tell you about three events in this period.

On 15 August, the feast of the assumption, George Haddad, a young married man of 30 with a seven-year-old son, had gone with his family to see his parents-in-law. They were all sitting at home and seemed sheltered from possible attacks, when a missile exploded in the street. A piece of shrapnel entered the young man's heart, killing him instantly. He has left a young wife and child.

On 25 August, in the middle of the day, a missile fell on a building in Jabrieh, an area where mainly poor families live. The explosion caused the death of five people. Several dozen were injured and dozens of houses were damaged.

On 26 August, Bassam, an eight-year-old child, was playing with his friends in the garden of the church when he was hit by a bullet in the head. He was an only child. The doctors immediately pronounced the child brain-dead, but his young parents could not accept this or come to terms with it and hoped for a miracle from heaven. The little boy stayed for days connected to the mechanical ventilator, dead but with a heart that was beating.

His mother Kinda, although she was unwilling to leave her son alone in the intensive care unit, came with her husband to Mass on Monday 29 August. She said to me: "This cross is really heavy for me." I told her that the cross was not only hers but also belonged to the whole church of Aleppo, and that we were carrying it together, with our hands in prayer not only for Bassam but for the whole country, which now lives as though it were in a state of death.

After long days of the greatest suffering, on 30 August towards sunset the news came that Bassam's heart had stopped. It was a sign of mercy for him, but above all for his parents who had remained at his bedside with their hearts broken.

The next day, the day of the funeral, was a terrible struggle for me against the chaos and desperation that tried to reign in the heart of the mother, the father and the whole community. I spent the morning sitting opposite the parents, next to the body, to prepare them to be calm during the funeral so that it might be a moment of prayer and communion with their son.

It was also a difficult struggle with the scout groups that competed with one another to organise large demonstrations in the streets, making noise and playing instruments. It was a very hard battle with the relatives who wanted to carry the body through the streets, dancing as though they were at a wedding party, to express all their grief and despair. In the end, the Lord of peace prevailed and we were able to celebrate the funeral calmly, in an atmosphere of meditation and prayer.

In the homily, facing the crowd that filled the church, I spoke of the image of God that is reflected through the life of Jesus: a tender, good, and merciful God in love with men, who knows perfectly well how to carry them, even through the evil of this world. This image of a good God, I said, is sometimes demolished subtly and sometimes directly by the enemy, especially at dramatic moments such as the funerals of our loved ones. They are terrible temptations against faith in a good God who, although he is omnipotent does not prevent the evil linked to the freedom of man but can make good out of evil, life out of death.

Despite all the initial sadness and agitation, during the funeral we were given a peace that could only have come from above. During the condolences at the end of the day, we were even able to put a smile on the face of Bassam's parents and relatives.

The funeral spent in prayer with a spirit of meditation was a miracle, accepted and witnessed as such by all those present; it was a testimony of the resurrection of Christ.

Aleppo is like this: a city of destruction and death. I am not even sure whether it still exists. Every day there are stories like these, the grief of parents who lose their children or of children who lose their parents. The people are always in a state of shock and are suffering enormously. We friars take on the daily cross of the people, a cross that is becoming heavier and heavier. We spend our days in pain and toil, visiting hospitals, accompanying the dying, celebrating funerals, visiting damaged homes and homeless families.

Our heart is attentive to a very difficult challenge, that of keeping the flame of baptism alight in the heart of each of the faithful of Aleppo, in the middle of this great storm that has been raging for many years now and threatens to destroy the city.

What happened in Italy, with the death and injury of hundreds of people, opened new wounds for me. I feel for them as though they were my own parishioners. From the very second we received the news of the earthquake, we offered holy Masses and our prayers and suffering for the Italians who died and for their families. We did this because we are united. It is not a coincidence that we are the members of a single body; it is a choice made by the Lord and a great responsibility for charity and communion.

9 October 2016[22]

Walking through the streets and corners of Aleppo – my city has been in the continuous storm of war for more than five years now – I see ruins everywhere, not only of demolished buildings, but also of people who have been destroyed from a human point of view. Not long ago, a lady knocked on the door of the monastery, asking to meet me. Her name is Lara, she is a 30-year-old widow and mother of two children. She needed to open up to someone. Her family had come to Aleppo in search of work. Now she is in need. As well as the psychological suffering caused the loss of her husband, the responsibility of bringing up her children weighs on her. They have so many needs she cannot meet, she feels like a dove with a broken wing and she cannot carry on.

In Aleppo, there are a lot of widows like her, who are in need of everything. They come looking for us every day. There should be a project of spiritual and material assistance for their needs, but there is only a small association which looks after about 40 war widows, taking on their problems in a praiseworthy way. Of the many people injured by the war, these widows are among the weakest. According to a survey, there are about 2,000 widows in Aleppo who belong to the different Christian rites. Looking after them is really a great challenge for a martyred Church. Every time the Old Testament refers to social justice, the Lord mentions widows, orphans and foreigners, prohibiting that injustices be done to them. In the New Testament, St James talks of supporting widows and orphans in need.

22 This article by Father Ibrahim was published in *La Porta Aperta*, a supplement of the newspaper *Avvenire*, with the title, "With the hands of the Lord in the night of Aleppo".

In our pastoral work, we are alarmed by another worrying sign: children and young people born in heartbroken and broken families. In general, the Oriental family is an example of a solid unit, in which marriage vows are kept and lived serenely. However, the number of families that no longer live according to this tradition is increasing. Many children grow up in difficult family situations, in homes where violence and quarrels between the parents reign. Others live with only one parent, because the father and mother have separated or because one of them has emigrated, often without ever sending any news. These minors are the future of the church and of Syrian society, but they carry the wounds of the past with great bitterness. In the family, they have nobody to count on who really follows the path of the faith. Their negative interpretation of reality affects their relations with others, of whom they are often afraid. The more these children grow, the more they show a relational imbalance. Most of them are intelligent and of good character, but they feel pessimistic and have little confidence in the future of their family. Speaking with them, as well as with fathers or mothers who live as though in the shadows, the wrong image of God can be perceived. Not having experienced tenderness and equilibrium in the relationship with one or both parents, these young people cannot understand the affection, the tenderness and the mercy of a God who loves personally, who has given himself for each one of us.

Thinking of the women, children and youngsters with troubled stories, my parish priest heart fills with compassion. They are my children and they need to be loved, accompanied, guided and supported, as I would also like to be if I were in their position. I have always liked the strategy of Jesus in John's gospel. What characterises him is personal encounter. He speaks at length with the Samaritan woman, although she tries initially to get rid of him quickly. It is the same with Nicodemus, who is troubled by the uncertainty of his faith and the concern that he still cannot grasp the thought of the Master. With the blind man, Jesus comes near, intervenes and heals him, and then he meets him and welcomes him. These are long encounters in the middle of the many engagements of the Master.

Similarly, in the encounter of Jesus with the widow of Nain, related in Luke's gospel, there is so much tenderness, so much compassion: an action, the move to stop the coffin, then the word that is born out of love, a love that restores life to the dead man, and afterwards the attentiveness of personally giving him to his mother. This is our pastoral style. Each person is precious, especially the weakest elements of a society like ours, now exhausted by the war. At every encounter, the same meeting of Jesus with the people is repeated, an encounter of listening, full of affection, emotion and tenderness.

Our activity in the jubilee year, and in a time of war and suffering, takes place both levels: the spiritual one and the human and material one. So each fish is caught personally, each lamb sought because it is precious and is brought back to the flock, to the community. These are our priorities: compassion, having the same feelings as Jesus, the desire to accompany widows, children and youngsters along the path of faith. It is a pastoral style of mercy, one that the Lord taught us and which is applied today in Aleppo, a city which cannot have the mercy of the international community.

PART XII

Between November and December 2016, the fighting in Aleppo became even fiercer, approaching its final epilogue. Amid growing uncertainty and fear about the future, hope was never lost. People awaited the end of a nightmare, an end which, despite everything, they could begin to glimpse.

23 November 2016

In the past few days the situation in Aleppo has been very difficult. Two days ago, a school in the government-controlled district of al-Farqn in the west of Aleppo was hit by a missile launched by the rebels. Many children died, others were wounded. Nowhere is safe. We do not know when or where the next missile will fall. Though we do not understand, we are united in prayer, we trust in the Lord because he is our hope.

Early December 2016

It has been a long time since my trip to Europe,[23] but many engagements in this situation of great change have kept me from writing to you. I say great change because we, the inhabitants of Aleppo, all feel that we are facing a new phase. We have entered the eye of the cyclone and we no longer know what may happen. As I write to you, I can hear very heavy bombing, the rumble of planes and missiles falling very close to me.

The previous phase had begun when I was in Italy: heavy bombing of our areas, accompanied by the arrival of armies and weapons that have almost filled the west of Aleppo. It was only a preparation for the offensive by the regular army, supported by its allies.

....

23 Father Ibrahim is referring to a trip to Italy between the end of October and early November 2016.

In the current phase, since the beginning of December the army has been advancing to take the eastern part of the city back from the rebels. This is the most difficult time for us: we can no longer count the missiles that fall on us. Only the day before yesterday 35 missiles fell in the area of Giamilieh; one hit the Saint Louis hospital of the Sisters of St Joseph but did not explode. There were also many deaths and injuries in our area and in the eastern part of the city, where very heavy bombing has started on the shelters of the armed groups. There will certainly be civilians in the middle of it all, paying the price of this absurdity.

The other evening, seeing the gravity of the situation, the central government in Damascus ordered the closure of all Aleppo schools for a week, confirming our recent fears. The city is shut down, its people out of breath. It is really shocking to hear children saying out loud and with tears in their eyes that they are afraid of dying.

5 DECEMBER 2016

A piece of news from government channels informed us that the area of the cemeteries had been secured. So we went to see ours. From afar, we saw that the wall surrounding it had been destroyed. Going in, we were able to see the great damage. It had actually been an area of fighting: the fighters went in and out of the cemetery to spy on the other side or to launch missiles. The house of the caretaker was in a terrible mess. Several tombs had been opened. The most heavily damaged part of the cemetery was that reserved for the poor and for foreigners. The poor in this Syrian crisis have paid the highest price and not even the deceased poor buried in the cemeteries have been spared.

I went there with a trusted engineer of the parish and so I told him what the priorities were. The workmen immediately got down to work: the wall was the first thing to repair, but all the tombs that had been opened and the bones scattered all around also had to be tidied up. Then a general plan of the cemetery would have to be drawn up and the plan of the tombs, which had been lost, recreated. The caretaker, killed in front of the gates some time ago, would have to be replaced.

10 December 2016

This morning, after a long time, the weekly meetings of the bishops and vicars resumed. This time we were hosted by the Maronites. There was a long list of topics to discuss.

As evening was approaching, four bombs fell in our district of Azizieh. One fell right on the monastery of the Jesuits, but we thank the Lord that the damage was only material. I immediately went to visit the two Jesuits remaining in Aleppo (Father Sami and Father Ziad). I told them that they were welcome to come and stay at our monastery, but despite everything they preferred to stay in their home.

Tonight the fighting is continuing without stopping. It is like a nightmare from which you can never wake up. But Sunday is full of joy and hope.

PART XIII

On the evening of 22 December 2016, the regular Syrian army declared Aleppo a "safe city". A new phase started for the population. But even if the missiles stopped falling (although not everywhere), the emergency situation continued. The city and its inhabitants were still on their knees, but hope was rekindled and people started to talk about rebuilding.

22 December 2016

After long talks between the army and the armed militia, the military groups handed over their weapons and left the east of the city. As soon as the news came, all the mosques summoned the faithful to celebrate and the churches – the ones that still had a bell tower – rang their bells. A dream has come true three days before the birth of the King of Peace. Everybody is celebrating! It is the best present that we could ever imagine. Only God could make it come true. We asked him for this gift and he answered our prayers. *Magnificat anima mea Dominum!*

23 December 2016

We learned that the missiles have continued to fall in Hamadaniya, causing nine deaths. Lord, pity! Our hearts are concerned about the safety of our churches in the Christmas period. In Iraq in the period after the war there were car bombs and explosives everywhere. We hope that such a blood-filled scenario is not repeated. Lord, the people can no longer tolerate it. We, their religious guides, are also finding it hard.

Christmas Day

From the darkness, the light was born. Christmas is indeed nothing other than light, which then produces joy and hope. In spite of the darkness that continues to envelop Aleppo, the light of God is shining.

In our church of St Francis, as in all the churches in the city, Christmas Mass took place without the background noise of bombings and shootings for the first time in five years. We are convinced that this is the result of the fervent prayers of the united hearts of many children all over the world. Every day, we receive messages from many different countries: Ireland, Japan, Egypt, Ukraine, Slovakia, Italy, Poland, the United Kingdom, Spain, Mexico, Argentina, the United States etc. All the children, but also many adults, are praying for peace in Aleppo. Prayer is what has brought us this miracle of peace.

At the start of the eucharistic celebration, the children (lots of them) joined the procession with the celebrants, carrying the lit candles, a sign of our vigilant hearts ready to meet the newborn child.

The universal prayer was said in four languages. We prayed for our beloved country, that the child Jesus with his power make the grace of peace and stability shine on it. At the end of Mass, the children accompanied Jesus in a procession towards the crib, which this year was given the shape of a map of Syria. Jesus was placed there, a sign that the birth of Christ is a new hope and a light for the city of Aleppo, Syria and its inhabitants. When it was time for the final blessing, the people clapped for a long time and very loudly, a sign of great joy and emotion.

The Masses and feast days in our parish community have always had an ecumenical character: many faithful from other rites join us.

Christmas Mass was the occasion for a fraternal meeting in the joy that reinforces our belonging to the church. In this period, we fear the kind of attacks by extremist groups that recently occurred in Egypt.[24]

24 On 11 December 2016 a bomb on the complex of the Coptic Cathedral of Cairo caused 26 deaths.

We thank God for all the joy of this day. We thank him for the fact that everything took place in peace.

A Christmas of rebirth

The fact of being able to celebrate Christmas in peace in Aleppo was something that we did not even dare dream of. We feel that this year the Lord with his coming has allowed Aleppo to be born again; there is a rebirth for all of us.

I don't know whether to speak of a new birth for Aleppo (and for each one of us) or of a resurrection. It was not only a thought I had; a person came up and whispered to me, "On this feast of Christmas, I feel as though we are celebrating Easter. I feel as though we are experiencing the resurrection."

At the same time, another feeling, which seems contradictory, is that of a bitterness that cannot be hidden. Firstly because in this, as in every war, there are no winners and losers. All the sides are losers. The proof is before our very eyes; our city is now destroyed. Secondly, so many families who lived in the east of the city have come to our western part with nothing, in the terrible cold of the past few days, hungry and thirsty. The reason we did not decorate the church outside is precisely because we thought of our Muslim brothers who had to leave their homes and are continuing to suffer.

27 DECEMBER 2016

This morning, Catholic bishops and priests met to resume the monthly meetings that had been suspended for a long time. The idea of a synod for the Catholic clergy came from several quarters. A detailed study of our Christian situation is necessary from several points of view. Based on this, we could create guidelines to accompany our mission. Everyone agreed and a small board was set up to prepare it.

Remembering the Christian martyrs

At 5pm in the church of St Francis, the scene of many of the ecumenical celebrations in Aleppo, the eucharistic celebration took place for all the rites of the city in memory of the Christian martyrs who have died in these years of crisis. The families of 247 martyrs of all ages were present and it was not rare for families to have lost more than one member. The celebration took place between the feast day of St Stephen and that of the Holy Innocents, as if our martyrs were included in their company. During the prayer of the faithful, we prayed for all the martyrs, including many children. We prayed that their blood might water the seeds of peace all over the world. We prayed for Aleppo the martyr city, for Syria and for the whole world. At the end, we placed our sorrows and wounds into the hands of our mother Mary; she, the mother of the martyrs, accompanies us in perseverance, she is our consolation, the balm for our wounds.

There was an atmosphere of meditation and sadness in the church. The black worn by the families of the victims mixed with the white, the red and the violet of the flowers that decorate the church on these festive days. It is like experiencing the same contradiction experienced by the holy family: joy for the birth of Jesus and sorrow at the news of Herod's massacre of the children.

In Aleppo, though we celebrated Christmas there are very many people and families who have lost their dear ones. They, like the mothers of the innocent martyrs, continue to cry. Their tears have not yet dried.

29 December 2016

Close to our Muslim brothers

Before the holidays, and after the liberation from the nightmare of the missiles, I refused to show any sign of the festive period outside the church. My heart was turned towards many of our Muslim brothers who, in the last battles, had had to abandon their homes in the east of Aleppo and were now living in various fringe areas of the city, like Gibrin and Hanano.

During all the homilies in the Christmas period, I spoke of them to the people. We feel a great joy because the terror has ceased for us, but there is still great sadness in our hearts because the brother close to us is suffering of cold and hunger. Let us start with prayer and then Divine Providence will point out the path to take to lighten their suffering. I know that Caritas and the Jesuit charities for refugees have taken steps in this direction. As for us, we were going to wait for Christmas to be over, with all the engagements that it entails, before devoting ourselves to humanitarian help for these refugees.

Suddenly, however, a stimulus arrived through a telephone call from Msgr Mario Zenari, Apostolic Nuncio to Syria, who as a real pastor and representative of the Holy Father told me he had a sum of money ready and another that might arrive the next week for the church to support the refugees from the east of Aleppo. I told him that as a Franciscan, I was willing to help in the aid work somehow. I have become an expert by now in spending for the poor. I wonder, though, with everything that we are already doing in the fields of pastoral and humanitarian service, with all the commitments we have taken on, if we will still have time for this. Yet I am certain that there will be some minutes left over, or some hours, that we can dedicate to Jesus' suffering in our Muslim brothers.

A letter to Pope Francis[25]

Your Holiness,

We, the Latin parish of St. Francis in Aleppo, thank you for your message addressed to us in your letter for the celebration of the 50th World Day of Peace.

The first of January 2017 is, by divine harmony, the first Sunday of the month. In our parish every first Sunday of the month at 11am, we celebrate the eucharist with children for peace in Aleppo, in Syria, and in the world. Father General Michael Perry OFM and Father Francesco Patton Custos of the Holy Land in their message for Advent for this year, have transformed this initiative into an invitation to the whole Church throughout the world and to all people of good will to organize the moments of prayer each first Sunday of the month in communion

----

25 The parish of St Francis in Aleppo has always had a special relationship with the Pope, who has on several occasions shown he is close to it. Pope Francis personally answered this letter personally a few days later (c.f. p.89).

with us.[26] The aim is to intensify the efforts to stop the war and the suffering of the civilian population of which the most vulnerable are the children. Some of them know no other life than war. Others were born under bombings. They suffer enormous psychological pressure, malnutrition, lack of water and electricity, adequate medical care, and are cold and hungry. Rarely does a smile appear on their faces. Suffering comes through in their frightened eyes. They live in distress for years. They wake up under the sound of explosions, bombs, and rockets in response to the fact that you never know where they will fall. And always to the detriment of the civilian population, without distinction.

[...] Holy Father, we thank you for the theme of your letter: nonviolence. Throughout this war, we seek ways to be ambassadors of forgiveness. Jesus taught us this attitude by his example. He has forgiven his killers. We ask him to heal us by his grace, so we will become the people who "banished violence from their hearts, words and deeds" and like St Francis, the patron of our parish, we can be in turn an instrument of reconciliation. Every time we meet together, we also pray for those who hit and kill. When everything that it is possible to do is not successful, "convinced of God's love and power" we use the only effective weapons that we have: love, truth, and prayer.

Holy Father, we thank you for being on our side. We thank you for your prayers and for your calls to heads of state and governments to stop this war. We assure you of our love and prayer and we ask you to bless us and send us a message that we would like to read on 1 January during the eucharist with the children of our parish and, through live transmission of this Mass on the internet, to children around the world.

---

26 "We want to propose to all our communities the 'Children praying for peace' initiative. It began as an idea from the 'Aid to the Church in Need' project, and we wish to join it as the Order of Friars Minor, and to relaunch it on an international level on a monthly basis [...] Our Parish of St. Francis in Aleppo, which has been strongly affected by the tragedy of war and which has been tenaciously anchored to its hope for peace, has already joined the initiative. From Aleppo, we are now sending out our invitation to the whole world" (from the Letter of the Minister General and Custos of the Holy Land, 27 November 2016).

1 JANUARY 2017

As on every first Sunday of the month, there were a lot of children present for the Mass for peace. They were still a little sleepy because the day before they had stayed up with the parents – some until 4am – to welcome in the new year. They wanted to express their joy at celebrating, for the first time in many years, without fearing bombings or shootings. The war has calmed down, even though it makes us sad to know that there are still many people who are suffering.

I asked the children, who has been very close to us in all these years, and continues to be close to us? Who prays for us all the time? Who speaks about Aleppo and Syria to the world every day? The children guessed immediately, because it is a person who is very dear to us. Pope Francis! Then I announced to them that the Holy Father had sent a message in Arabic in response to the letter sent to him.[27] At these words, the church packed with children exploded in a thunderous applause full of joy! We read the message together. It is full of love for us, of concern, compassion and understanding but also full of encouragement, support, hope and closeness. Just as a father and mother suffer in seeing the pain of their children, the Pope is suffering for us, for Syria and in particular for Aleppo. Through his words, we feel that he is close, as though he lived in our midst.

We left the church with our hearts full of gratitude and joy for this gift that the Pope gave us at the start of this new year: his special blessing. But we are also grateful for his message that contains important challenges for us at this time: the challenge of trusting in "the child of the manger who, being born in our hearts and in our homes, can heal our bleeding wounds and heal our suffering bodies and souls" and the challenge of believing that "Jesus can transform our painful experiences

....

27 "I willingly join you in the prayer to the child in the crib, the King of Peace, so that he can spread his peace, which is above all intelligence, to your country, to your city of Aleppo and the whole world [...] I am close to you with my presence and my continuous prayer for you and for your beloved country. I give you, your parish and all the children of the world, my Apostolic Blessing! (extract from the letter of Pope Francis, 31 December 2016)

into points of strength and hope, the tests of violence and pain into encouragement towards reconciliation and healing."

2 JANUARY 2017

Waking up after a long sleep

Inside me, there is a list of questions for which I have no answers. What is this post-war period in Aleppo going to be like? The war is actually not yet finished, because there are areas where the missiles continue to fall. Living conditions are the same. The people of Aleppo are prostrated by poverty, hunger, thirst and the lack of work.

Does the government have a plan for reconstruction? Would it help us to rebuild the churches (and the mosques) that have been destroyed, that are a sign of great hope for the people, or will we have to take care of it? Where can we get the money?

How should we behave towards those who are suffering and are still living as though in camps? Will living conditions improve? Regarding aid, we know with certainty that we have to continue giving emergency aid. At the same time, we must think about rebuilding.

I, and the whole of the Church with me, feel like someone who has woken up after a long sleep, someone who has finally been able to lift his head after a storm in the desert and looks at the horizon. We look and we are aware of everything but we do not really know where to begin.

"I am like a weaned child with its mother, like a weaned child I am content" (Ps 131:2). I am sure that it is not us who do things, but the Lord. It was not our hand that freed us from death and war, but his hand. There is nothing we can do in the face of the drama of a country, but he, who works miracles, will mark out the way.

I then pray for an act of trusting abandonment to the Lord, through the best loved prayer of the heavenly Father, that of Jesus on the cross: "Father, into your hands I commit my spirit" (Lk 23:46). I too, Lord, commit Aleppo, Syria and the whole world to you. You who have preserved us in these long years of war, act as you can in favour of your poor creatures, not only Christians, but the Muslims as well.

5 JANUARY 2017

Since the start of the year, we have had a non-stop influx of people coming to Aleppo one after another: first the Greek Orthodox Patriarch, then the Syrian Orthodox Patriarch, the Armenian Orthodox Catholicos and Msgr Georges Abou Khazen. I went to greet each of them.

On 2 January the heads of the Christian communities in Aleppo met. Yesterday the heads of the Christian communities and the Muslim leaders had a meeting with the Prime Minister and six cabinet members.

A *difficult reconstruction*

This last appointment was very special and important. It was special because it was the first time that we, the religious leaders, were invited to meet the Prime Minister in private. It was important because we got many answers, positive and negative, to questions of vital importance for the inhabitants of Aleppo.

It was very interesting to hear the Muslim religious leaders speak of a desire to renew the religious discourse and present religion as completely distinct from fundamentalism. They are worried about the challenge of educating and training children and young people, as well as about getting new school books. Everyone supports education that excludes fundamentalism. Several Christian religious leaders spoke. They also insisted on the challenge of education, especially on the need to make everyone grow up with respect for diversity. Their words also focused on very concrete things related to the living conditions of the people, who are paying the price of the war.

The Prime Minister himself answered many of the questions. We are still in a state of war, he told us. Electricity, therefore, will not reach Aleppo for another year, or when ISIS has been chased out of the northeast. The water situation will not improve. We must not expect the state to rebuild houses or provide compensation, because it does not have the resources. They may look at some of the oldest churches or mosques. They will do something for the industrial, productive part of the city and try to make it easier for Syrian entrepreneurs to return to Aleppo.

The Latin community questions itself

After this series of meetings, one important meeting had yet to take place: that of the priests of the Latin community of Aleppo. We met with Msgr Georges, who gave everyone an account of all the other meetings and opened the discussion. Many vital points emerged.

Living conditions have not improved since the end of the bombings. There is no work; the city, which was an important industrial centre, is completely paralysed. We agree that emergency aid has to continue and so do the plans for reconstruction. The church has to take upon itself the responsibility to help families. We must not look around and judge the shortcomings of others or other communities who are not doing anything; we, with the blessing of the Lord, can carry on and fulfil many needs to look after all the Christians in Aleppo.

Lastly, in the name of the universal church, we have committed ourselves as consecrated men and priests to give our Muslim brothers more help in this phase, both in the east and the west of the city.

INTERVIEWS, MEETINGS AND ACCOUNTS

How can a person accept, against every reasonable consideration, to be sent to Aleppo during the bombings? What future can there be for Syria after so much violence? How should a Christian behave in front of the enemy? And where is Providence if we only see the cross?

This second section of the book contains public speeches Father Ibrahim gave in Italy, via Skype from Syria or in interviews. They are pages which have a different flavour to some of the letters in the first section. They are written for the Meeting in Rimini, the faithful in many Italian parishes, newspaper readers, television or radio audiences – people Father Ibrahim does not know directly. These audiences are curious but perhaps also less informed about the situation of Christians of Syria. Father Ibrahim thoroughly explains what is happening in Aleppo.

These speeches are not written in the heat of the moment, with the immediate urgency of relating news about the war, or as an emotive reaction to a dramatic event. They are mostly more detailed reports, in which the events in Aleppo are reread in the light of faith. These reports are obviously the result of much reasoning, reflection and prayer.

Here, we find not only the war and its consequences of bloodshed, but above all the search for a Christian meaning for the cross which the Syrian people are carrying. Father Ibrahim applies this search for meaning without hesitation to his own life, going over the stages of his vocation, remembering his encounters with the Lord who in the end was waiting for him in the most unimaginable place: Aleppo.

14 MARCH 2015[28]

The start of my mission in Aleppo

I always wanted to study, ever since I was young and since I was ordained a friar. But obedience to the Lord and necessity have taken me far from academia. After competing a degree in dogma in Rome, I enrolled for a PhD but, before I could discuss my thesis for the degree, my superiors told me that it would have been difficult for me to continue with the doctorate because there was a great need in the region of the Custody of the Holy Land, in particular in Syria. I answered that, in the face of need, I had nothing to argue. This way I started to prepare myself spiritually and physically, but I did not know exactly for where; only later did they start to talk to me about my destination.

There are different options and there are many needs; everywhere we friars are present in Syria there is a great need for people. There is a shortage of friars. It would take about 10 to meet all the needs, especially in this difficult moment of suffering. In that period, in prayer and in silence, I asked the Lord for two things: for him to send me to a difficult place where I could do what was within my capabilities and for him not to let me see needs without being able to face them.

My superiors then offered me the chance to go to Aleppo, telling me that the city was devastated and the population was suffering enormously. The parish priest, after years of tension and the pressure of war, was exhausted. They asked me for my opinion. I answered that I had no views: "You decide and I'll go." I had no reaction, I only prayed. Then, slowly, I perceived that the Lord's will did not match my thoughts, even my reflections and meditations before the most holy sacrament. The Lord's will was something completely different; the heart of the good shepherd was turned towards his sheep.

This way, with a simple but deep obedience of the heart and of my reason, I threw myself into reality. I also enrolled in the doctorate. I was given the opportunity to continue my studies from afar, should it be possible. Then, however, I completely immersed myself in the situ-

28 Video-link with the Church of Gesù Divin Lavoratore, Milan.

ation, praying to the Lord for the people that I was to meet in Aleppo, before even getting to know them. I asked everyone I knew to pray: consecrated and lay people, my parents and my family. After less than 12 days, with firm and clear resolve, I suddenly found myself here in Aleppo to start a new mission.

The drama of everyday life

In the past few days, we have only had half an hour of electricity a day. Last week, we did not have any water for nine days running. From the fourth day onwards, we started to switch on the large electric generator, draw water from our well and open our doors to the people, who came immediately with buckets to take water to their homes. Not having water means not even having anything to eat. It is shocking to see elderly people, who have nobody, and children carrying heavy buckets and receptacles. They queue alongside young men and women for a few litres of water.

Worst of all, however, are bombs falling on homes. We are about 150m from some armed militia who, out of revenge or hatred, launch gas canisters and missiles at the innocent population and at churches as well. Many bombs have fallen around our churches, which are targets. The militia kill people in their homes and people passing by in the streets.

There is a flood of suffering, despair and bitterness due to all this death. As a reaction, people have been running away, trying to avoid this whole area; they go to other churches in different parts of the city, even though they are not always safe, until the wave of sadness passes. Then life slowly goes back to normal.

This is what happened recently when a canister landed very close to our church. The gas canister broke all the upper windows in the building, which fell on the faithful during evening Mass. A youngster and a man died, both Christians who were shopping in a store nearby. After the grief of the funerals, the tears of many people and the presence of all the clergy of Aleppo, the days pass and fear subsides again. People try to live normal lives.

Several parishioners ask us existential questions. For how long, Father, will we be put to death one at a time? For how much longer will we stay here? Can't you send us all away? Can't you do more for us?

The cost of living is rising, due to the collapse of the Syrian pound, which leads to the dramatic increase in poverty and in the number of those who take advantage of this situation.[29] Everybody comes to our charity association. Those who were very wealthy in the past are now almost penniless, having lost their workshops, factories, shops and houses. In four years of war, they have used up all the assets they had and they have gone from rich to poor. It is surprising to see wealthy people used to dressing in very expensive clothes come dressed so well to ask for help at our door; they have clothes, furniture, a home, but they do not have food to live on. In the difficult times of these days without water, it was touching to find that people smelled. Well-educated and refined people would come smelling badly, because for nine days they had not been able to have a shower. We are now helping about 300 families, and the number is increasing all the time.

Then there is illness. We see many cases of certain diseases, such as of the liver, caused by air full of microbes and viruses. This year, the flu has been very widespread and has affected all of us. It only passed after a month of very vigorous coughing. The people are also getting physically weak because of the absence of medicines: non-professionals in the city are trying to help the many people who are ill.

Recently, we have also discovered dozens of partly destroyed houses in which people continue to live. Whole families with children with nowhere else to go stay under the missiles and bombs in houses with no doors, no windows, with a damaged roof, or even no wall. We are trying, with minimal resources, to relieve their suffering and that of the sick: those with tumours and chronic diseases, the abandoned, the terminally ill. In these cases, we have to be close to them, almost as though we were their parents or relatives. We follow their cases at every stage.

The eyes of faith and hope

We have no future prospects. There has been a proposal by Staffan de Mistura (United Nations Special Envoy to Syria) to solve the conflict in Aleppo, but it appears that the militia have not accepted the truce and the state of affairs between them and the government forces, as far as we can see, does

29 C.f. p.14

not augur well for the future.[30] four years of war have already passed. We will enter the fifth, then the sixth and the seventh. We do not know how long it will last. Many young people are fleeing to Turkey and Lebanon. Many academics and people of education leave for work of no prestige and without prospects. The elderly, young women and children stay with us.

With the eyes of faith and hope, we always feel, however, the certainty that we are experiencing labour pains; this suffering is preparing a better future. Only with the eyes of the faith can we see something good for the present and for the future, ours and that of our parishioners and fellow citizens of Aleppo and the whole of Syria.

The position of the Christians

Christians are not willing to enter the conflict. They do not consider taking up arms after having seen what happened to the Lebanese Christians who took the road of violence during the civil war there. Initially, the Christians of Lebanon took up arms to defend themselves from the Druze and the Muslims, but afterwards they ended up fighting one another and lost everything. Here, in contrast, most Christians have chosen to suffer, to be the yeast for a better future and, where possible, an instrument of peace between the parties in the conflict. Christians have always tried to get on with everyone; they have not fought or said that only one side was right. They also made an effort to drive the government to take action or improve the situation, but without weapons.

Something has to change in politics, but fighting each other will not change anything. The militia are, however, very divided; most of them come from other countries and are not ready for a dialogue. They seem

....

30 The offer – put forward in February 2015 by the Special Envoy of the UN to Syria, Staffan de Mistura – included a six-week suspension of the fighting in Aleppo, with the aim of opening a humanitarian corridor. De Mistura started a dialogue with President Bashar al-Assad, working out "part of the solution". Since 2014, De Mistura had been working to establish local truces (confined to specific parts of the country) and to achieve a progressive reduction of the fighting, in order to create pacified areas where someone could arrange the first humanitarian interventions and establish a political discussion between the parties. Aleppo was one of the cities in which this local suspension of fighting was to be attempted.

to have come here only to destroy. When they go through a part of the city, they destroy everything, even pharmaceutical factories or factories making baby formula. As a consequence, it is really difficult to speak about dialogue, except in limited contexts.

There is also widespread suspicion of others, because we know that some seeds of fundamentalism are present in the hearts of many of those who live with us.

Christians also continuously experience the haemorrhage of emigration. Every day, I sign many baptism certificates, certificates of unmarried status and confirmation that people ask to leave the country. Many young people flee to avoid military service. For the future of the church and of the state, we try to bear this collapse of society but we don't know for how long we will be able. As the church and as the consecrated, with the force of prayer and charity, we nevertheless try in every way to stop this daily disintegration.

One of the difficulties that we face as a parish is no longer having any idea of the number of families in our parish. We know nothing about many of them. We try to be strong, to gather our faithful, to convey more faith to them, to encourage and help them, and to go on, day by day, hoping that tomorrow will end our suffering.

The importance of charity and concrete signs

As the parish priest, I align myself with Jesus' way of carrying out the mission; I act with mercy in my heart and I let this mercy guide me. Perhaps the strongest sign that people perceive and love to see is that a parish priest, friar or other priest, is willing to give his life for them. Our faithful feel that this love is genuine. Not because of words, but also because of gestures of charity, they feel that their only security lies in being closer, going to church to pray, listening to and following what we are telling them through the word of God.

Just after I arrived, I spoke at length during a homily about the importance of confession and reconciliation with Christ. At the end of Mass, the other friar told me in amazement that many people had gone to him to confess. I understood how ready the faithful are to listen and to follow. Perhaps suffering erases hardness of heart, purifies intentions and people, enlightening them. This is a consolation for me. But I am also aware that many people are unable to reach us and perhaps are dying, or perhaps their faith is dying. I also see the evil that has been generated by this war; many souls have been lost and no longer have the strength to follow their path of salvation. We often no longer hear from these people, who have perhaps been unable to save their lives.

Christ's love and man's answer

Yesterday, after the via crucis, we celebrated Mass and I commented on what Jesus said about the greatest commandments: "Love the Lord your God with all your heart and all your soul, and with all your mind and with all your strength. The second is like this: Love your neighbour as yourself. There is no commandment greater than these." (Mk 12:30-31). I added a reference to the first encyclical of Pope Benedict XVI, *Deus Caritas Est*, and explained that nobody can love without first being loved. We are not the ones who take the initiative of loving. First of all, we have experienced the love of Christ and it is because of this that we answer.

Illustrating the signs of God's love, of the cross and of the sacrifice of the eucharist, I also spoke about the many people of good will who pray for us. Although without means and without knowing us personally, they give what they have to support the Christians carrying the cross in the Middle East, and in particular in Syria. I told my parishioners: "I know of many actions of this kind, which show how much the Lord loves you. It is your turn now to answer, loving not only your brother or your son, but also the enemies who are persecuting you."

Prayer is our support of faith and hope. Without the prayers of many friends abroad, we, the consecrated and parish priests, would not be able to continue this mission. This also applies to all the Christians here who live through terrible trials. The Lord makes us do things that are greater than ourselves. We friars have nothing; we try to help the people, we fast and we have reduced the money spent on our food to a minimum. The charity we receive performs many miracles and it is not the charity of money but of Jesus Christ who makes us feel his love. So, above all, we are not asking for economic help but for prayers, which for us are like air to breathe, consolation and sweetness.

The value of the Christian presence in Syria

I have often asked myself: must we be so close to Aleppo and the Middle East? Why don't we all leave and go to Europe, or somewhere else? I answered myself: goodness knows how many martyrs have shed their blood to plant the seeds of the word of God in this Arab land and culture.

How many martyrs have suffered so much just to establish the roots of Jesus Christ here? For these sacrifices, we must have the strength to oppose and resist. We have to remain because our presence is a mission that began with the blood of the martyrs and perhaps will continue with more blood and more martyrs. It is Christ who stays here and it is his light that illuminates these peoples through our blood and our suffering; therefore, even with the threat of the bombs, we must not abandon our homes and villages.

The church still suffers a great deal today to reach China, while for example it only succeeds in having a small presence in India and the path in this direction is still long. We, who are already here in the Middle East, must not give up. We have to persevere, if not for ourselves, then for the future generations, so that the name of Christ is always present in these lands and adored in the various places of worship.

15 March 2015[31]

The confirmations took place this morning and luckily everything went well. At the end, shaking hands with the parishioners, the bishop and the other friars, we all said: "We thank the Lord because today the bombs spared us." This alone is a miracle for us.

Here in Aleppo we are experiencing a nightmare that never seems to end. Every passing day requires greater and greater effort. Every day we include four or five new families in the projects of the parish charity association. Every day we see episodes of incredible suffering. We try to do what we can, to be close to the people, suffering with those who suffer and crying with those who cry.

31   Video-link with to the parish of San Michele, Magnago, Milan

The experience of the gift of the self

I have reflected a lot on why the Lord wanted me here in Syria, on what this experience means in my spiritual path as a friar, as a consecrated man and as a priest. Meditating, I have intuited that God wants to give a pastoral approach to my life, to let me enter the depth of pastoral life with the people. He wants me to experience giving to the suffering lambs, to have a special, long encounter with his suffering flock in Syria. So I give myself up to Providence.

I understood that it is the Lord who guides my steps, as he does with each one of us. Through this new post, he wanted to test me, just when I was about to complete my studies and my path seemed to be mapped out. In return, with the docility of the Holy Spirit, not mine, I let myself be guided. It was not difficult and I did not think about it for long.

Some people told me that returning to Syria would have been too dangerous and that I should have said no and finished my studies, but I answered that I did not have the strength to refuse a request that I felt so strongly and deeply in my heart. The force of the Holy Spirit also drove me to pronounce words that I had not even thought of. I felt a special courage and tenderness. It is the tenderness of those who can truly experience obedience, even when they do not understand with their reason. I believe I have passed this test which the Lord gave me and I think that he is training me through this contact with pain. I feel that many things are maturing in me and that I am growing in this very beautiful but difficult experience.

Recognizing the face of suffering Jesus in the other

You need immense courage to face the needs here. I think of the terrible cold we had this year or the lack of water these past four years, which hit periodically and without notice. For a week, even a fortnight, people live without a drop of water in their homes. We friars have learned to have a shower with only a litre of water, or by heating only a small amount, or with cold water. Terrible. This makes me reflect on how much waste we produce in terms of natural resources, electricity, water and food.

With regard to food, too, we have decided to live like the poor and to experience concretely what hunger means, remaining without meat or fish, eliminating lots of things that are not necessary and trying to live only with the minimum. It is our meditation at the moment: how much waste we produce, perhaps even without wanting to.

One day, a woman came to me and, almost tearing her clothes, told me she had two small hungry children and for days had nothing to give them. She was afraid that her children would go and steal, or do anything at all, just to get food. It is only when we really feel hunger ourselves that a situation like that really becomes comprehensible.

Perhaps what supports us in these situations is remembering Jesus saying that he was thirsty on the cross.[32] He still suffers today. He is not only thirsty but also hungry, cold and in pain. So, recognising Jesus in these people makes it very easy to go to them and console them. I feel that it is Jesus' suffering on the cross that I am meeting every day, in every inhabitant of Aleppo. What we have before us is the via crucis of Christ in which we, in particular we friars and priests who are the front line with the people here, are invited to participate.

The effort that leads to hope

At times it is not easy to share or transmit hope. It is often very difficult to do so in the face of episodes of death or of people screaming or swearing out of grief. Often at first we have to submit, to be even spat upon, then with patience and humility wait, listen and, in the end, help. Only later do the people come back to thank the Lord or show a new hope that has opened up in them. Here is an example of this experience.

A few days ago, a young married woman came to the parish office and started cursing and saying very harsh words against the church, blaming our secretary. They came to get me and I immediately started to pray to the Holy Spirit because, in situations like this, I find it very hard to keep calm. I met the woman, who started to use very strong words again against the church and the friars. She told me that she had been

32 "Later, knowing that everything had now been finished, and so that Scripture would be fulfilled, Jesus said 'I am thirsty.' A jar of wine vinegar was there, so they soaked a sponge in it, put the sponge on a stalk of the hyssop plant and lifted it to Jesus' lips. When he had received the drink, Jesus said, 'It is finished.' With that, he bowed his head and gave up his spirit." (Jn 19:28-30)

neglected by her husband for many years and lived in a house that had been destroyed. I understood from her eyes that she had gone through a series of psychological and nervous shocks.

I tried to speak but could not, because she kept interrupting me all the time and establishing a dialogue was impossible. Then I asked her where her husband was and why he was not with her. I asked her for his phone number and I called him, telling him to join us immediately so that we could confront the situation together and try to find a solution. I tried to calm her down, promising her that we would do everything possible. She slowly agreed and left. Then, in the street she started screaming again, losing control of herself. I phoned her husband again, insisting that I meet them at their house. On my way there to ascertain the situation, I prayed. I discovered then that one day when the woman was at home with her husband, a bomb had destroyed the only room of the house. I prayed with them and tried to help, offering some money.

Yesterday, after reconstruction and repair work, the woman came back to tell me, "Father, a new hope has been born in our hearts. We are incredulous. It is a new birth for us. As people and a family, we already feel it, we feel such joy." We thanked the Lord together and promised to meet again to glorify God when the work was finished at the house.

In conclusion, often communicating hope is not immediate or automatic but, when the facts are laid out hope comes on its own, without having to be transmitted. It comes from above, but through material care. Today I perceive that the style of my pastoral life here, just like that of all the parish priests in Syria, puts help before the word. We can speak of Jesus only after helping people.

Something similar took place when we were preparing 29 people for confirmation. Some of them were already adults who, in the past, had neglected to receive the sacrament. During the preparatory meetings, we explained to them that Providence had covered all the expenses and that they would not have to pay, so the number increased. The catechesis was also easier when it was made clear to them that they would not have to pay any expenses.

This is the slant that I feel I have to give to my parish service: the perspective of real charity which comes before the sacrament, before the explanation of the word of God. After having shown mercy to people's lives, it is much simpler to communicate Jesus.

The community of friars: life in communion and continuous conversion

As a community, we are also experiencing an important conversion. Although we had already taken the vows of poverty and obedience, with the passing of the years there is the risk of choosing prosperity and taking many things for granted. On the other hand, here, when we talk about the expenses of the monastery or about those for our daily life, we realise that this suffering is training us again in the school of Jesus and St Francis. When money is available, everything is determined by it, whereas when there is none you have to reason differently. I perceive this as a sign of our conversion. We must not think about the buildings, embellishing the monastery or the church, or enlarging the premises. We must no longer worry about the stones, but concentrate only on the living stones, that is, people, because they are the ones who really need to be looked after.

On many occasions in consecrated life, there is the temptation to construct, beautify or improve the premises. This aspiration is not wrong, it serves the faithful. However, sometimes we attend to these things before we attend to the people in Aleppo. Our monastery and church can be bombed at any time and so we are more realistic. We say that we should not put all our energy into improvements, but only into helping and sharing the lives of those around us.

I see that the clergy of the various Oriental rites are also taking a similar path. Some have lost all their churches and no longer have a place to celebrate Mass and the sacraments. They have suddenly left their spaces, addressing the population more easily. They have started to abandon their safety and now go to visit homes to meet families and pray with them.

In Aleppo, it is more natural to live a real conversion and in this I see the intervention of Providence in our path as Franciscans throughout the Middle East, but especially in Syria. I perceive how the Lord uses all this inexplicable pain to distribute a greater good, a special grace: the grace of conversion and a return to the origins, according to the teaching of St Francis. He recommended that the friars not own anything, but live free of everything in order to concentrate on their mission, with the heart of a father who waits for his children.

Interpersonal relations and the value of service

The situation in which we are living also influences relations in the friary. We have no alternative. We live together so we pray together, we suffer together and we face difficulties together. The suffering of Aleppo and of the whole of Syria almost forces us to embrace one another and not dwell on superficial details or minor problems. We establish real dialogue and because of this, we are face to face with grace.

Authority, therefore, is not a means of imposing oneself on others, rather it is an authentic service. Our presence here is not for the sake of prestige, but it is a chain that binds us to greater responsibility and greater suffering. Faced with the request to come to Syria to be in charge of a monastery or a diocese, the human logic of today would refuse, for so little prestige is not worth the effort and grief. Here, however, we understand very well that our task is that of washing feet, of glorifying the cross. Our charism is increasingly deepened with the poor, the poorest of the poor. Ours is a community in mission: friars who live their faith together, on the path of the Lord's service for our lesser brothers.

Grace generated by suffering

The anguish that we feel every day has also not only changed us but our people as well. Before this war, I remember that when I spent summers in parishes or when I went to visit my family, I saw ever greater arrogance, haughtiness and avarice. As soon as I arrived in Aleppo, on the other hand, I realised that something had changed in many hearts, making the people purer and more beautiful. Many who before were far from the church have started praying again.

There is an Arabic saying: "The more a carpet is beaten, the more it is clean and bright." When we speak about suffering, I repeat to my faithful: "See how pure you are today. Maybe you do not realise it but I am trying to transmit to you what I observe as a pastor. With your suffering you become more beautiful because we, the Christians, are like carpets. The more we are persecuted, the more beautiful we become."

The greatest threat is not persecution, but prosperity; it is not by chance that every time the Acts of the Apostles mention the persecution of the first Christian community, immediately afterwards there is a reference to the flourishing of the church and to the increase in the number of the faithful. I am a witness of this.

Many people far from the faith, or oscillating between faith and atheism because of the chaos, have had terrible nervous breakdowns or have opted for choices that are definitely wrong and detrimental to themselves and their families. However, I see that this suffering is generating good in those who sincerely believe and long for conversion. God, in his grace, brings out of the evil a good that is greater than suffering.

We are ready for everything, including martyrdom. I am not afraid of death, but slowly you enter into the perspective of every day, of today, and you no longer think about the future. This is also a grace. "Each day has enough trouble of its own" (Mt 6:34). We try to resist despair, doubt and incredulity, and to follow faith and hope.

Giving unconditionally

In the parish, we try to rely on Providence, asking the Lord to think of his people. I can witness to the fact that Providence has never failed us. I have never asked the Lord to intervene, because he has always done so at the right time, with concrete answers.

Yesterday, as I was meditating on my parishioners and their many shortcomings in faith and on the moral path, I wondered, in the light of the word of God, who among us is worthy of being loved. We are not worthy of being loved because we have done nothing to earn the right to be loved by the Lord. St Paul says, "But God demonstrates his own love for us in this: while we were still sinners, Christ died for us" (Rom 5:8). We also follow the same logic, apparently absurd, of charity that does not consider whether the other is worthy of being helped or not. It is the Lord who has given us this teaching and we do not follow other rules.

It was rather difficult to make the members of our charity association understand this concept, because those who have worked for many years in this field have mainly adopted criteria of selection for their charity, giving the priority to the poorest. On the contrary, I wanted to transmit Jesus' point of view on divine charity: nobody is worthy. You give without reflecting at length, without conditions. Where there is a need, you give and that's that.

We do not intend to accumulate wealth, saving money as security for the future, because perhaps here there will be no future. The best thing is always having an empty safe. This is the path of St Francis and Mother Teresa, but it is also the one, I think, of every parish priest who has learned from Jesus to love his people. We are faced with so many needs but we also feel the presence of the Lord who is constantly with us.

1 MAY 2015[33]

To build the church, the Christian, like a new Adam, has to work without sparing himself, with effort and sacrifice. The church is in continuous construction, based on the cornerstone that is Christ and on the foundations of the apostles. It grows through the life and work of all its members, summoned to make a real spiritual sacrifice. Every breath of love, even the tiniest offering from the faithful to the Lord, is a sacrifice of praise to God to build his church.

The spiritual sacrifice is the gift of one's life to the Lord, an offering that the Father appreciates, and continuous praise. This is why Christians who suffer every type of persecution out of love for the Lord and as credible witnesses of the faith are a precious treasure for the whole church. They are the greatest manifestation of the profound meaning of Christian life: total and unconditional donation to the Lord. This testimony, even in the form of martyrdom, is a precious gift for the church which, in turn, is consolidated both spiritually and physically in its visible body. The church, nourished by these experiences, gains the strength necessary for its growth.

Today Aleppo, a city which in the past was an important industrial centre, is a set of ruins, a place where terror reigns and where there

33 Delivered during a prayer vigil for Aleppo at the church of St Francis in Grosseto, Tuscany

is a shortage of everything. Several times I was asked why despite the dramatic situation people, mothers and fathers, decided to stay, facing insurmountable difficulties and challenges. To this question, one mother answered that emigrating today is very expensive and that she could not afford to. Another said that she did not want to emigrate because she did not want to be a burden on the country where she would go. A young father, on the other hand, answered with another question: "Who would I leave my parents to? They are old now and need care and assistance. In any case, they could not tolerate the great change of culture and life in a society other than the one in which they have lived so far."

Another family said that, despite all the terrible things we are going through, the Lord is concretely present here and now. He looks after us and gives us our daily bread. Why leave? A third young father replied that it was the Lord who planted the tree full of the fruits of Christianity in this holy land, trodden by the apostles Paul and Barnabas, generators of the first Christians. For this father, the presence of the church in Syria is a sign of divine will. Looking at the big picture of a greater mission and testimony, we cannot afford to leave this land, he stressed, because it would be a betrayal of the will of the Father, an unforgivable flight from the testimony of the cross.

23 AUGUST 2015[34]

One word describes the situation of the Christians and the whole Syrian population: chaos. We are living in total confusion. The city of Aleppo and its outskirts are divided into dozens of parts. Chaos reigns, because there are many groups of jihadist militia, each of which controls a part.

An unstable situation

We lack everything: safety above all. We are under a continual shower of bombs that the militia launch everywhere. Over time, various parts of the city have been completely destroyed, as is the case with our neighbouring area where now there are only ruins.

34 Talk entitled "A reason to live and to die: martyrs of today", delivered during the Rimini Meeting for Friendship Between Peoples 2015

INTERVIEWS, MEETINGS AND ACCOUNTS

The bombings are getting closer to our monastery. They have hit the street parallel to ours, even touching our very beautiful church of St Francis. Many people had already left their homes and fled to other parts of the city. We are right in the line of fire and we do not know when the church might be hit.

These groups of terrorists, unfortunately, have hit hospitals, schools and homes not only with gas canisters, but also with missiles that have a considerable destructive impact. The haemorrhage continues and sows death, mutilation, emigration, terror and despair.

The price of food is very high and it is very difficult to find meat, milk, cheese and butter. The poorest have stayed with us. Wealthier people all left during the first two years of the conflict. Healthcare facilities are becoming poorer and there is a shortage of medicine; many doctors have left the country and private clinics and hospitals lack medicines.

There is also no water. This drama has intensified in the past month and a half. Some jihadist groups are in control of the pumps that send water to the city and they pour it into the river to prevent the population from drinking. There is no electricity or water in homes. In six weeks, there was only water on eight days. We are terribly thirsty.

When these essentials are missing, how do you convince a Christian to stay? Why should he? Many cannot continue living in Syria and there are Christians leaving the country. It is like living in a scenario from Revelation, a text I meditate on almost every day. Horses arrive – the horses of death, famine and plague – and then, totally unexpectedly and suddenly, they turn in another direction or they want to run another lap (Rev 6:1-8). The situation is very unstable.

Listening to the cries of the innocent

One must have patience and carry the cross every day. But you also have to react with concern, paying continuous attention to the Spirit that is blowing, to the needs of the people in the streets, not only the Christians but the Muslims as well.

When a woman knocks on our door to ask for water, it does not matter whether she is veiled or not, what matters is that she is thirsty. The same applies to hungry children and the people who run away from the bombs and need safety. Here, humans are deprived of their dignity. My brothers and I suffer greatly, not only from personal grief, but because we see human dignity hurt and stolen.

Our answer is creative. By listening deeply to the voice of the Lord and the cries of the innocent we understand how to react. We ask for, live and feel generosity in ourselves, linked to our Christian nature as consecrated men and priests, willing to even give our lives. We open the door to all those who seek us, day and night. We must really learn from Jesus who thought about others during the hours of his crucifixion, about the future of Mary and John, about the salvation of the good thief and all those who were near him. Despite his suffering, Jesus was worried about saving not only the whole world through the work of redemption, but also the man suffering next to him. He was also able to forgive those who crucified him, who were not even asking for forgiveness. Our response is generated by faith and by the example of Jesus.

Sometimes, I laugh inside when I think of myself because I, a lover of books and advanced theological studies, am here in Aleppo being a firefighter, a nurse, a caregiver and, lastly, a priest. But this is the real experience of the consecrated man and of the lay person who feels called to serve and build the church. One day in the street a person carrying buckets, some of which were visibly dirty, stopped me. I offered to take them, but he did not want help: "Father, you risk dirtying your habit!" I answered that our habit is made to be used in the service of others.

Opening up to dialogue

We are in a great crisis; fear reigns and there is enormous suffering, among Christians and some Muslims who are ashamed of what is happening and for this reason try to avoid talking about fundamentalism.

We live in uncertainty, but it does not matter when and how it will end. What is important for us Christians is being able to bear witness to Jesus Christ, not worrying about saving ourselves. We have to help everyone reach a solution (even a political one) and act. But our first task is to bear witness to Christian life and to carry the cross lovingly, forgiving and even thinking about the salvation of others. We are a few yards from the terrorists who are sowing death, mutilating people, destroying everything, yet every day in our community we offer our suffering for their salvation, we pray for them and we forgive them.

A Christian lady who lives near our church (in an area where most of the families have always been Christians) and is beloved in the parish was recently complaining that her neighbours had changed. Many Muslims rented or purchased the former houses of Christians. She perceived that something significant had changed – the atmosphere of the streets, people's expressions – and she felt uncomfortable about the presence of so many non-Christians. I answered her: "Isn't it perhaps the Lord who allows people to change the environment around us, so that the perfume of Christ can reach others? Couldn't this be a wonderful mission that the risen Christ is asking of us? We have so much to hand on."

I have learned from the history of the church that a Christian is not afraid of anything. He does not fear comparison, diversity, subjecting the Bible to other types of study and disciplines, or opening up borders. In short, he does not fear dialogue. He has a very great treasure in his heart and so can dialogue with everyone freely, without losing his nature; indeed his nature is made up of the exchange of riches. This is what we Christians, in the midst of the semi-destroyed city, are trying to do with everyone, and often we succeed in conveying values without even using words.

Peace of the heart

A little while ago, a Muslim who has always worked for us, came to me and whispered in my ear: "Father, I, who have been all around Aleppo and seen what is happening elsewhere to the wells, am amazed to see how the people come to draw water from you. They do it with a smile, with great peace in their hearts, without quarrelling, without fighting, without raising their voices. You are different, full of joy; you are able to share with the others, even the Muslims, and do it in peace."

Being a Christian in Aleppo has a profound value. We do not give up; we love, forgive and witness more. Christian life is always a narrow path with many difficulties but numerous victories. We experience grief and death, but not fear, because we have the strength of the resurrection. We know that our sufferings have a meaning of redemption for us and for those who kill us, indeed for the whole world. We are right to act as real Christians and be radical in living our faith with joy and peace.

Signs of resurrection

Every day in Aleppo, I see many signs of resurrection. For example, being able to celebrate daily Mass without interruption from the beginning of the crisis until today with the doors of the church always open is already a miracle for me. Still being alive is also a miracle. We are able to better appreciate the gift of life, as well as of water and health. While we value things that we do not have, we can still give thanks. We are increasingly full of gratitude to God who fills us with his gifts.

Fundamentalism makes us ask essential questions. Is the path we are on the truth? How great the search for God is. We give thanks for the power of charity, forgiveness and the service that we can carry out. Many of our Muslim brothers thirst: those who knock on our door, those who ask questions about Jesus Christ and those who come into church to listen to the word of God. Thirst is reawakened. We are sure that this is a sign that the risen Jesus is present in the persecution of Aleppo.

20 JANUARY 2016[35]

New missiles in our part of the city

On Saturday 16 January, at around 4.15pm (three-quarters of an hour before the vigil Mass) the weapons went back into action in Azizieh, where our parish is, after a short-lived truce. Five missiles were launched against our area, just a short distance away from the church of St Francis, which had already been hit on 25 October 2015. They fell on houses. The buildings are very close to one another. Missiles thus cause great devastation both to homes and building façades.

I was in the parish office with some of the people who help us and in the porter's lodge there were a number of people waiting to speak to me. Suddenly, we heard explosions. The first missile went off about

35 Phone message during "Appeal to humanity", a prayer initiative for the persecuted Christians in Iraq and Syria organised by the Nazarat Committee of Rimini

150m from the church; we held our breath and invoked Providence. After that, there were other explosions until a missile exploded closer to us. Instinctively, we all stood up and began to try understand where it had fallen. I phoned the families near where we thought it might have happened. Postponing talking to the people waiting, we followed the fire-fighters in the street.

Although I have seen many houses that have been hit, I was immediately overcome by a great bitterness and sadness. You cannot get used to so much evil: striking unarmed people in their own homes, especially the elderly, children and youngsters who were studying in their bedrooms. I went into every house and I prayed with the families who were in the middle of great anguish. There were no dead, but some people were seriously injured. More than anything else, the people had great fear in their eyes. While praying in every house, I thanked the Lord for the absence of fatalities.

As the hours passed and in the light of the next morning, the vast extent of the devastation appeared before our eyes: buildings gone, ruined houses without windows or doors, women and men who were trying as best as they could to put their homes in order. There were several levels of damage. Without a doubt, the most serious damage was to the people, who, totally overwhelmed, no longer knew what to do.

In the monastery, I immediately called the engineer and together we went back to see the houses. Most of the families no longer have anywhere to go and in these cases we have to give a concrete sign of hope, intervene straight away in the best way possible. Unfortunately, it is not the first time that missiles have fallen on Christians' houses causing these terrible scenes of ruin and desolation. We are forced to start assisting all over again.

The decision to remain

Though many Christians have already left the country or would like to but because they don't have the means remain with a deep-rooted feeling of frustration, I have also met many people and families who, although they already have a visa, have decided not to leave. They say that this is a holy land, watered by the blood of martyrs. Today they are nourished by the merits of these great martyr saints and it is their turn, and ours, to make our contribution to the faith of the future. To me, this seems to be the best reason for families staying.

As for me, I have been living in Aleppo since October 2015 and I have never felt, not even for a second, the temptation to abandon my mission. I was asked to come to Syria and I did so out of obedience. But I also chose this path and I follow it. I want to be a sign here of the presence of the Lord.

How the Christian community is perceived

Many citizens of Aleppo, Christians in particular, see the Syrian crisis as an opportunity for purification and preparation for a splendid spring-time of faith. There are however, two different points of view on the Christian community. Some fundamentalists see us as a threat; our very presence is involuntarily a source of challenge and rancour. In contrast, many other Muslim families find our presence precious and edifying; the Christians are a model of life, an authentic testimony to be imitated.

In general, our relations with Muslims are good. We have always been close to them and they are aware of how much good we do for them too. We are the first to help when there is a need. They know that we try to love our neighbour with all our strength and the Muslim families are pleased to accept our help. In daily life, the cross that we bear is the same and the problems of the high cost of living, the lack of water and electricity are identical for everyone; we feel in full communion.

The force of prayer

At the end of last Sunday's Mass, one of the altar boys observed, "When you arrived here, you were always smiling. Now you smile less." It was the third time that I had returned from a visit during which I had seen much pain; it was difficult for me to smile as I usually do during Mass.

Like in other parts of the world where there is disorder and chaos, the church's task in Syria is not a simple one. It must now take on functions that would normally fall to the government or civil authorities. What Christians and people of faith abroad can do for us is pray that the Lord give us the strength to continue. Prayer is definitely useful to make us feel like an integral part of the Catholic Church and not a forgotten branch. For us, it is a powerful force. In reciprocal communion, we grow together in the faith and thus also improve in witness.

27 FEBRUARY 2016[36]

It is a miracle that we are still alive here in Aleppo. In the past few days, life has been a little harder and more difficult than usual.

In the part of the city controlled by the regular army, there were numerous bombings of homes from 4 to 15 February, in particular in the areas where there is a high percentage of Christians. Many missiles fell, during the day and at night. We have families who have lost their homes or whose homes have been very seriously damaged. These families have very deep wounds. Today we committed to taking 43 families under our wing, which means 43 houses to repair. This is our way of helping people out of a nightmare.

Stories of intense grief

The worst thing, without any doubt, is not a home that has been destroyed or damaged, but the fact that several people have lost their children or parents under the rubble. There are many wounded in the clinics and hospitals and we do not know whether they will survive or not.

One Christian family's 15-year-old son died under the rubble due to a missile which hit the house, razing it to the ground. The father is now in a clinic and the mother, who does not know yet that she has lost her son, is in another. Her face is disfigured and her facial bones damaged, she has lost an eye and the doctors do not know whether she will still be able to see with the other one. The woman has to have a long series of operations. Every day, going around the houses and hospitals, we collect stories like this one. We continuously receive emotive shocks that make us participate in the intense grief. We are human and so totally immersed in it. This is part of our ministry: "Rejoice with those who rejoice; mourn with those who mourn" (Rom 12:15).

----

36 Video-link with the San Giovanni Bosco Sunday school of Abbiategrasso, Milan

The need for a truce

One of our most important projects is linked to the constant lack of water. There has been no water for a month. Despite all our efforts, we are not able to take drinking water to the houses of all the families. There are people who live on their own and lots of ill people who have had operations and have nobody to look after them afterwards. We also look after a large number of children who are aged under two. Everyone needs water.

There is no fuel and we no longer know what to do to meet the many needs around us. We have heard of a truce that we hope will really come into existence and will last. We also do not know whether the road connecting Aleppo will be opened again. Because this only road is closed, people are now beginning to feel hungry and there are already many people ill with liver diseases. Many people have diseases linked to the unhealthy atmosphere, polluted resources and viruses.

The gaze of the heart

We friars keep praying and encouraging people to have trust. The Father, tender and merciful, will not allow his people to perish. As we do not see a future with our eyes, we close them and we look around with the eyes of our heart, which are also the eyes of faith. We stare, not at the high and threatening waves that surround us, but at the calm face of Jesus. Walking on the waters, he looks at us and encourages us to walk with him without drowning (Mt 14:22-32). We can proceed firmly, relying only on knowledge and on Divine Providence, which we continually experience. It is Jesus himself who said: "Look at the birds of the air; they do not sow or reap or store away in barns, and yet your heavenly Father feeds them. Are you not much more valuable than they?" (Mt 6:26). We try to live with this awareness, not sparing our energies or the little money we have. We also never stop praying.

The mortgage emergency

In this period, we have another emergency, that of bank debts. Every day, one of our lawyers meets several families, offering them sound advice to face the bank debts with which they are burdened. These meetings allow us to remain better informed of the situation of each family and, more often than not, we can help pay off the debts. We have been able to help about 80 families that risked remaining without a roof because they were not able to meet mortgage payments that were years in arrears. Obviously the figures involved are far too high for us. Despite our efforts, hundreds of other families are still waiting for help.

The debts are like a missile that come crashing down on a family, destroying it. A high bank debt that has accumulated means that a whole family is evicted, has to sleep in the streets and risks breaking up. To avoid this, we have decided to intervene, although at a considerable economic expense with a dose of courage. Great courage is needed to help families with this delicate matter.

Different forms of assistance

We friars coordinate about 18 volunteers who operate in various fields. Sometimes in reception we deal with 25 difficult cases a day. Most of them are people or whole families who need every practical kind of aid.

A few days ago, we distributed 140 boxes of foodstuffs. A box for each family, relieving them somewhat from shouldering the burden of survival. This distribution will continue for all our 624 families of the Latin rite, but we are thinking about extending the service to 300 Catholic Armenian families, who are totally without food aid. We try to include people from other religious confessions as well.

The priestly ministry – confessions, celebrating Mass even in the afternoon and giving daily homilies – is an essential part of our mission. We also make pastoral visits to homes and hospitals. We meet the ill and administer extreme unction and viaticum when they are close to death. There are also many people who contact us for spiritual guidance.

Sometimes at the end of a long day, when the internet works we have to answer messages to try to tell the world about our plight. In this way we feel less alone. The suffering and countless needs we encounter every day increase the risk of not having time to speak in detail, especially with friends, about what we are experiencing therefore of not receiving in exchange the comfort of their presence in incessant prayer.

The gift of health and the abandonment to Providence

One day, after several visits, I went to two families who live on the fifth floor of a building. To reach them, as there was no electricity, I had to climb the stairs. Climbing step after step, pensive and out of breath, I found myself thanking the Lord for my health. It is a precious grace without which I could not be here among his children in Aleppo, reaching them even in the highest and most inconvenient apartments.

We must never tire of thanking the Lord for health, energy and the charity that consumes us in help for others.

Paul's first letter to the Corinthians (1 Cor 10:1-6; 10-12) speaks to all Christians of Aleppo. Referring to the path of the people of the first alliance in the desert, the apostle exhorts Christians to avoid the diseases of this people, that is the lack of faith and lack of abandonment to Providence. These lead to the sins of arrogance, pride and gossip-mongering. On our path in the desert, we must never let ourselves be defeated by discouragement, the ancient spirit of arrogance, pride and gossip-mongering. These attitudes hurt our Lord the most. We must not lose even a fragment of the trust that we always have to put in him.

22 APRIL 2016[37]

In the past few days, despite the talks in Geneva, the violence has unfortunately increased considerably.[38] The negotiations have not reached any agreement and so the jihadist groups and the armed troops around

37 Talk organized by a youth group linked to the parishes of San Donato e Carpoforo of Renate Brianza and San Martino di Veduggio con Colzano, Monza

38 Negotiations started on 14 March 2016, two years after the failure of the talks started by the UN in Geneva, which had ended without any political agreement. The objective of the talks, conducted under the supervision of Staffan de Mistura Special Envoy of the United Nations in Syria, was to put an end to the hostilities and create a government of transition which could promote a new constitution. In the final phases of the talks, the representatives of the main forces present in Geneva issued contrasting declarations on the state of the process of transition, while the United Nations asked for a commitment by the USA and Russia to save the truce.

Aleppo continue to launch missiles against the population. We can hear the bombings over our heads and afterwards we always receive the news of how many people have been killed, how many are buried under the rubble, the number of children, injured and elderly who cannot move and so on. Every day, there are several episodes of violence, but the result is identical: suffering continues indefinitely.

The difficulty of meeting basic needs

We can no longer meet basic needs. The water was cut off today and we do not know when it will return. This is happening more and more often with electricity too; since it went off two weeks ago, it has not come back.

We need doctors specialised in various disciplines. Today, for example, we needed a psychiatrist and a doctor with expertise in respiratory problems. But very many doctors in the forefront of their field have left the country. More often than not, we face illnesses for which it is impossible to find a solution in Aleppo.

Two days ago, we visited a 60-year-old man who has a very serious respiratory problem; in order to survive, he urgently needs oxygen day and night. When he went home from the hospital his family bought an electric generator but despite their best efforts they found it impossible to get oxygen. Even when large generators can be obtained to distribute some electricity in homes, they do not work at night. For this man, who also has serious heart and kidney problems, all that is left for him to do is await death. There are thousands of cases like this. Everything here contributes to increasing the suffering of the population.

Industry is at a standstill: the factories are closed, many men are unemployed, many shopkeepers no longer have their stores. How can we give even a small sign of hope to all these people?

The answers of the church to the countless needs it sees

As a community, before speaking about Christ, we try to provide the help people need, beginning with food and health. We also help by buying a little electricity from the generators in the streets so that families can have at least one light on in their homes and, if possible, turn on the television in the evening to follow the situation. At times, richer families can even make their washing machines work, which requires more electricity. In all other cases, washing has to be done by hand.

There are, however, countless other needs. A week ago, for example, a missile fell on a building and five apartments were seriously damaged: each apartment lost two rooms, which were destroyed together with the balconies. Luckily there were no dead or injured. Only Christian families lived there and the building was in a wholly Christian area. The many children present survived without injuries; it was a real miracle.

Visiting the damaged homes, we realised that many families no longer had any clothes or furniture, which were buried under the rubble. So helping them continue to live decently was not only a question of providing for the repairs of the house. We managed to help some families settle, either by renting other apartments or starting reconstruction work. Many homeless people do not even consider fleeing to another part of the city; nowhere in Aleppo is safe. Therefore, starting to reconstruct and repair immediately is, without a doubt, a real sign of hope.

The water emergency continues

The very serious water problem continues. Too many houses, unfortunately, do not have a large capacity tank on their roof. From 500 to 1000l would be necessary to store water but most families, who could never have imagined going without running water for months, are unprepared. We have supplied as many families as possible with 500l metal tanks. Until now, with an enormous effort, we have been able to distribute more than 400 tanks, but about 900 families are still without.

Every day we encounter elderly people who live on their own and cannot go up and down to a high floor to draw the water necessary for drinking, cooking and other basic needs, women who have to give birth or have a small child and need a lot of water, men who can no longer bring the buckets to the fifth or sixth floor because, as there is no electricity, the lift cannot be used.

Other aspects of our humanitarian aid

To date, we have been able to eliminate 217 families' debts but to solve the problem completely, we need the same amount of money again. Each month, we distribute food to 900 families. Each parcel contains good quality, nourishing foods both for children and the elderly: cheese, chicken, rice and other staples. We also provide for small children who need nappies and other things, and we help in the cases of families whose children have problems like autism, malformations or disabilities. We look after many widows and women who have been left alone by husbands who have fled abroad in the hope of a better future.

Healing with the word of God

Our pastoral work has a very special impact. We heal with the word of God. People need food and medical aid, but they also need the sacraments and the word of God, which is a source of nourishment. We have baptised many babies and celebrated children's first communions and youngsters' confirmations. Recently, we have also started a course for engaged couples. We hope that more and more young people will want to marry despite the tragedy of this senseless war. It is important to encourage them to walk in the natural path of Christian marriage, towards the edification of the small domestic churches that are families.

We friars continue this service with joy, fully trusting that the countless problems, difficulties and fears will not stop us. Every day, we suffer with those who suffer, because we feel that we belong to this country.

My sources of strength and creative charity

There is one thing of which I am certain. Although I am a friar and a priest, I am first and foremost a Christian who has experienced God in his life. My mission cannot be conducted without a deep relationship with God. I often receive positive feedback from people, but I am aware that the strength of this charity is not mine; if I did not draw on the strength of God, I could do nothing. For this reason, prayer is essential for me. During the eucharist, I feel as if I am in heaven. The same thing happens during my personal and communal prayers. It is from there that I draw the strength of creative charity, which appears not only through ordinary ways but also through new and extraordinary ones.

My encounters with people also give me strength. Yesterday towards evening, for example, despite the intense bombings I went to visit three elderly people. I gave them communion and the unction for the sick. Going home to the monastery that night I felt much stronger than I had when I set off to visit them. The encounter with the suffering – as Mother Teresa of Calcutta, St Francis and all the missionary saints understood – gives enormous strength. The more I give of myself, the more this strength grows, making me increasingly joyful and satisfied.

These are my sources of support: the direct relationship with God at daily Mass and in prayer, and the encounter with the suffering. In serving we realise that we too are served by charity which gives unreservedly.

The relationship with the Muslim world

The other, someone who is different from us, is always a challenge. Living with those who are different, whether in the family – I am referring to the relationship between husband and wife, parents and children – or in consecrated life, is a challenge. The important thing is to face up to difference and always try to build bridges. This is how we work with the Muslim world. We represent a challenge for them and they are a challenge for us. The same applies within our world. There are differences among Christian rites, just as we differ from the Muslim world.

There have been moments when, as Christians, we have felt betrayed by our Muslim friends. There are, however, many other Muslims, individuals and families, who have remained close, faithful to the principles of coexistence and solidarity, and who work together with us for the common good. Therefore, though we cannot easily forget negative experiences, as Christians we cannot dwell only on the negative.

We make every effort to behave, with them and with everyone, like Christians, as Jesus taught us. Then everything changes: when I do not adapt my behaviour to that of the other, his goodness or lack thereof, my only response becomes what my faith teaches me. As a consequence, we love and always pray for the other. How many times in our churches and in the community during the prayers of the faithful we have prayed for those who are bombing us. We pray, together with families who have lost loved ones, for those who have killed, those who are different from us. We do not only think of ourselves when we distribute food parcels, but of them too, because this is the teaching of Christ.

The power of charity

I am convinced that, like evil, good is also contagious and has the power to spread continuously. My experience in Aleppo confirmed this countless times. I try to surprise people with abundance, as the Lord does.

The strength of this charity has grown and now involves lots of people who before were shut up in their egoism. I see many who have grown more generous and I see this, for example, in the collection during Masses. We priests certainly do not demand anything of the parishioners, because we know the great need they are in. But it is surprising to see how people become more and more generous, offering the little they have for the needs of the poorest. With regard to the bank debt problem, for example, though we pay off the debts of many families, we have also been given house keys by some people who were leaving the country and still wanted to help the homeless.

Naturally, this generosity is not always the case. A few people have stayed shut up in their own world. But we can accept this, knowing that, at the same time, the majority of our faithful are more charitable today than they were before. This attitude fills our hearts with joy.

The absence of prospects and hope for the future

We are now plunged into the most complete chaos of all. We no longer have the perception of what is happening around us, we no longer know who to blame. We have gone beyond the phase of looking for a justification, identifying those responsible. We are no longer able to see a meaning in what is happening to us. We have a very poor view of what may happen tomorrow. We do not have any prospects.

Yesterday we heard several bombings; we did not know which side they were coming from, who was bombing what. Nobody gave us any information. Should missiles fall where we are, we would die. If they fall elsewhere, the next morning we have to try and understand where they fell. If it is near us, we have to figure out what happened and who we have to look for. Chaos reigns; everyone is fighting everyone else.

We have only one certainty: the Lord is suffering with us and this is the moment of the cross, of non-comprehension. It is not the time to ask questions, but to submit, rather, to deliver ourselves to God with trust. In these circumstances of extreme doubt and confusion, we only have to open the eyes of our heart and let it beat to the voice of our Lord, our guide. The leaders of the world offer us only contradictory positions and speak of a chaos which will continue indefinitely. However, listening to the friendly voice of our Father means being sure that beyond the present crisis, days full of joy and peace are awaiting us.

This is the logic of faith. We are perfectly aware of what is happening around us. Like Jesus on the cross, we suffer. The darkness continues, but in our hearts reigns the certainty that our faith gives us strength to resist, dream of a better world and, above all, start to build it now.

17 MAY 2016[39]

We have had no electricity or water for several days. Every day, someone is killed in our part of the city. Yesterday, for example, a woman was killed by a rocket as she was about to give birth, so her baby also died. A house was also burnt down, together with several cars. There were many other injuries. After many hours, a child was extracted from the rubble.

Living in uncertainty

For a while, the situation appeared to calm. But everything has changed with this new shower of missiles. We do not know when, where and how we may be hit. When you leave your home, you do not know if you will return. Most people are greatly disoriented. For students, both in secondary school and university, it is the period of exams, but their parents are increasingly doubtful as to whether they will continue sending their children to sit them. Many want to leave Aleppo, even though this means taking their children out of school after they have studied

39 Recorded for a meeting with the parish community of the Basilica of Santa Maria Nuova in Abbiategrasso, Milan

hard for the whole year. Many Christian families have fled without even knowing exactly where they were going. Everyone, without exception, is fully aware that Aleppo is no longer a city where they can live.

As a friar, despite the great danger, I try to live my days in the normality of service, leaving the monastery when I have to go and visit people in their homes.

Today I saw about 20 Christian families, including some people with serious problems linked to the trauma of the war. They are women and children who show symptoms of serious psychological disorders.

We are in a hurry every day; every day and every instant have rules of their own. We cannot plan our days because the service we perform is made up of decisions taken second by second and the same is true for those families who have to fight all the time for their daily bread. Here are some examples.

Before the bombing two weeks ago, we accelerated the distribution of water tanks, delivering hundreds of them to the families who were still without. Suddenly, however, because of the bombings we had to suspend everything; for almost two weeks, the volunteers have not had the courage to use the van for these deliveries.

While we are trying to carry on repairing homes, working continuously with engineers and groups of specialised people, a missile can hit and change the kind of work that we have to do. We have to welcome the many families who knock on the monastery door to ask for shelter, money and food. Only later can the repair of houses begin.

In addition to these jobs, naturally we have to continue our pastoral service, which also takes planning. It is May, the Marian month, and so there are evening Masses to celebrate, homilies to prepare and confessions to hear. We try to do everything well, never tired of having to run around from morning to night. We cope with emergencies, but our pastoral services are our top priority because they serve desperate people who need a word of comfort, a blessing or concrete help.

Contemplation and service

Ours is a life made up of work and contemplation. This was the subject of a meeting today with about 100 women from the Association of St

Anthony of Padua: contemplation and service, the roles of Martha and Mary, how the eucharistic sacrament relates to the washing of the feet. There cannot be a separation between the contemplative dimension and the action of service. Charity for our Lord is not in conflict with charity for our brothers. We would never have imagined this duality in our humble service.

Mary is our model. At the time of the angel's annunciation, the most intimate moment of her entrusting herself to God and her union with him through the Holy Spirit, Mary was able to go out of herself to serve her cousin Elizabeth. Mary, at the highest point of her contemplation, performed the most perfect form of charity towards her neighbour. Elizabeth had not asked her for anything; it was Mary's own initiative, a gratuitous act of charity, an act that developed from her profound contemplative dimension.

Today I was trying to explain this dynamic of our spiritual life to my people. It is a dynamic proper to us friars and priests and to all the people of God. Every day, here in Aleppo, we live a really intense life. The signs of this balance between work and contemplation, a balance which gives shape to our person, can be seen clearly. It is the fruit of salvation which sprouts in the heart like real peace and, as though by contagion, is also communicated to the lives of the people around us.

The miracles of Easter

We are witnesses of the miracles of Easter in the life of our people; they are not physical miracles but something far more important. Here is an example. On Easter Sunday, when four families (about 15 people) were visiting their grandmother, a missile totally destroyed the house, killing an 11-year-old and an 18-year-old.[40] Some people, including the man whose work supported the family, were seriously wounded. We friars immediately went there, trying to support them all spiritually and materially.

When the family later came to see me in the monastery, we thanked the Lord together for life and for death, for the fact that 13 people were spared and we entrusted all our existences to him. The mother of the

40   C.f. pp.62, 67

11-year-old then gave me a beautiful smile, and so did her brother who had lost his 18-year-old son. The woman made a very great impression on me; she was smiling and showed great peace. Looking at her, I thought, "Perhaps she is not yet aware of what has happened; she does not feel the grief that she will certainly feel in a few weeks." However, talking to her, she surprised me as she began to thank the Lord because 13 out of 15 people, despite the missile that fell on them, were still alive. She praised God because she was sure that the two youngsters cruelly killed were now in a safe place, in the hands of our Father.

The question I asked myself as I watched her walk away was: "How can this woman still smile only five days after the death of her son and thank God for what she has gone through in this atrocious experience of death?" The answer was that, among us in Aleppo, the light of faith is bright and always lit, despite the strong gust of the wind of violence.

These are the seeds of life that show the presence of our Lord in our midst and in the hearts of our faithful. We are nourished by the word of God, which always gives us great consolation. It edifies and defends us from the temptation of despair. The sacraments, the eucharist in particular, are our strength and joy. Fraternal communion also makes us every day a little more aware of what we are, the limbs of the mystical body of Christ. We experience that this communion, lived in suffering, unites us more and more to Jesus.

How the bank debt issue is proceeding

An update on the situation of the bank debt that weighs on many families: it remains an enormous burden for our weak shoulders. Today there are about 450 Christian families in Aleppo who have accumulated bank debt and who risk losing their homes.

Looking from the outside, it is often difficult to understand fully what the real needs are. We focus on food parcels, medicines and urgent operations. When, however, we speak in concrete terms about very large issues of a different nature, more often than not it is as though we are trying to stop large waves with only our bare hands. Despite all our good will and our certainty that our Lord never leaves us, all the (even economic) things that we have to take care of can leave us breathless. Personally, I have to take important decisions every day and, to be able to carry on, I follow our Lord who speaks to my heart. I do it with sincere faith but, at the same time, with quite a lot of difficulty and fear.

Finally, after paying a huge sum of Syrian pounds, we have been able to settle the debts of about 100 families. But there are still at least another 100. I often tell the volunteers (who help me with total trust and dedication), "Let's go on until the very end." After our intervention, some families are full of joy and say that they do not have enough words to thank us. We started with about 60 Latin families, but we could not restrict ourselves to them, knowing that families belonging to our sister Oriental churches (for example, Orthodox families) were unable to settle their debts. In time, I found myself involved in an exercise that was beyond my abilities. I therefore had to entrust myself totally to Providence, certain that the same Providence that had made me start my mission in Aleppo with little money and 600 Latin families suffering from hunger, would not abandon me.

We are sure that our Lord will never let us perish. His plan, not ours, will be accomplished for us Christians of Syria, and in particular of Aleppo. Our mission as Franciscan friars here is also his plan, not ours, and I have no doubts about this accomplishment because I feel it echo in my heart. Purely human considerations would never have made me undertake, for example, the project of paying off debts.

My experience with the Lord

To explain the experience I am living with the Lord as my travel companion, I use this image: it is like walking with a friend at the edge of a pool. At a certain point, my friend pushes me as a joke; I don't have a choice whether to dive in or not, because I have already fallen into the water. I experience this dynamic with our Lord very often. When he pushes me, I am already in the water. I have no choice.

Many times, both in the field of humanitarian aid and in that of spiritual and pastoral service, I have felt thrown in at the deep end of choices that I would never have made with my will alone. It has been a fundamental test for me, one which has left me consoled and gratified.

I continuously feel that the will of God always wins over mine and that my will always conforms to his.

In Aleppo we are in a profound crisis, but we are also constantly taking action so that the Lord's will be done. Never have I regretted help offered or any decision taken to serve those most in difficulty. I thank our Father because it is he who guides us and I am comforted by contemplating his extraordinary works.

23 MAY 2016[41]

A strike on the College of the Holy Land in Aleppo

Two missiles struck our College of the Holy land, in the area of the university (an area until now considered safe) and which in peace time was used as a recreational centre and home for vocations. We Franciscans in Aleppo run the parish of St Francis of Assisi, the branch of Er-Ram and the College of the Holy land. Er-Ram is a centre, which, with its school for the deaf and dumb, was always open to Christian and Muslim children. It has already been hit five times. Every time our brother in charge repaired the damages, new missiles destroyed all his hard repair work.

The College of the Holy Land is the place of extended projects and is open to non-Christians. It has brought together many groups of needy people: deaf and dumb, blind, sick children and groups of elderly people, Christian and Muslim. The parish centre of the area of Azizieh is very small and we have a large Christian community belonging to all rites, so we can carry out activities only for Christians.

The College of the Holy Land was targeted by two missiles. The first fell on part of our land that had been forcibly taken by government military forces to use as a centre of enrolment for military service, the second on a room where the elderly of the St Vincent de Paul old people's home usually sat for their afternoon recreation. These elderly people had been in a building next to the cathedral. When they were forced by the bombings to leave it, we offered them a wing of the College. In the green spaces of the College, these people were at last calm.

41 Interview during a short visit to Italy

As well as destroying the facilities, the missiles caused the death of a lady of 94 and the injury of two people, one seriously. The explosion was heard very loudly and there was enormous grief.

Christian families of Aleppo have always considered the College a green lung; they could go there for fresh air or to let children, who had no other green space, play. It was the only place with a large green area where the young people, unable to leave the city, could attend summer camps. We had started repairs and maintenance, but what happened shows that we will have to wait for peace and greater safety.

The disorientation of the Christian community

The Christian community is going through a period of darkness and uncertainty. Psychological illnesses and the number of people who are taking medicines are increasing, especially among women and mothers who are no longer able to sleep. The children, who are the weakest victims of this situation, find it hard to remain on their own for even a short period; they are often restless. They have skin diseases and symptoms caused by the terror they have experienced.

Families wonder whether to remain in Aleppo or to flee. They say that staying until now might have been the wrong decision. Many Christians are fleeing, especially after all the recent missile strikes on homes.

The flight, not always out of Syria, is often the result of the disorientation of families who are at risk of losing their house and work. They throw themselves into a world where they have nothing, no point of reference. Many children who had end-of-year exams have had to stay at home, while others, who have fled with their families, have lost their whole school year because they were unable to sit the final exams.

We try to welcome and help. I personally feel that my experience is turning me into more of a mother than father. Motherly, material care of the people sometimes prevails over spiritual guidance and admonition.

An appeal for peace

We love all the people who are in Syria, even those who are fighting against us, whether they are Syrian or not. We really want their ultimate good, their salvation. We pray not only for the wounded and for the innocent, but also for those who fire instruments of death at us.

Let's say stop to this war, to the hatred and to the violence. This is what I also ask, with all my heart, of all those who fire missiles, who kill so many innocent people. Today, in the jubilee of Mercy, there is room for them as well and the Father calls them to reconciliation with themselves, their brothers and with him. They should accept this invitation to return to their consciences and to try to stop the conflict, building bridges to create together what we call the Kingdom of God on earth.

26 MAY 2016[42]

I have to confess that, after all these years in Aleppo, one thing is increasingly clear to me: we have to carry on with trust, because it is our Lord who makes history.

In these years we have been struck by intermittent waves of violence. After each wave comes bewilderment, silence and surprise accompanied by bitterness, fear and terror. Many people who were determined to stay in Aleppo are won over by the idea of leaving everything and fleeing. But we cannot stop in the face of these waves of violence.

Our reaction to the provocation of evil

I was very impressed by something that the Apostolic Nuncio in Syria Msgr Mario Zanari said the last time that he came to Aleppo to meet the priests and consecrated men and women. The Nuncio told us that this crisis is a real provocation by the devil and that we, as the church, can respond creatively. This is really true. On the one hand, from the emotive and rational point of view, we are overwhelmed by everything that happens around us, by the violence and terror but, on the other hand, all of the evil can be a provocation for us. Prayer, communion with our Lord and between us Christians can generate an appropriate response, a firm and creative response. It is a reaction which, although it is ours, is not generated by us; we are driven by the Holy Spirit, by his moves and by his inspirations. It is a force of good that we would never have

42 Interview with Edizioni Terra Santa

imagined, to the point that we may surprise ourselves in what we do. This reaction also emerges very clearly from our people.

Yesterday, for example, the sister in charge of the children's summer camp phoned me. After missiles hit the College of the Holy Land on the night of 21 May, we had decided that whether or not safety was guaranteed we would continue with our plans. The summer camp is due to start and then there will be the celebrations for the end of the Marian month. On the phone, the sister was frightened and said, "Father, 230 children have registered, and we don't have any more space. We'll have to close the registrations." I answered: "Closing registrations and locking the doors is against the logic of God. Our Lord will know how to act and if we have to give part of our monastery for the children, we will."

Last year after a lot of work and two weeks into the summer camp, we got 200 registrations. Today, a week before it is due to start, there are already 230. The Lord's responses are visible, not only through us friars, but also in people's hearts.

In addition to the summer camp, we are continuing to meet the needs of people by giving food parcels to needy families (at first, there were 600; today, 2,000). We also distribute water and metal cans to store it. We secure health coverage, in particular for the elderly who need many examinations, tests, monthly medicines and operations. We repair houses that were hit by missiles. A network of mercy and charity extends further and further every day.

The urgent need for tranquillity and rest from the bombings

Despite everything, schools have remained open in Aleppo. There were of course difficult times before the start of the children's exams, but some families have been able to let their children finish the year. Others have moved to Latakia on the coast, even only for a few weeks, because they desperately needed rest. In the face of this great need, we started a project in Slonfeh, a resort between Aleppo and Latakia.

Slonfeh is a mountain village, traditionally very popular with people from Aleppo. We Franciscans have a small facility there with rooms to sleep in and a church. It is usually used by youth groups. Seeing so many cases of families with psychological wounds and children in difficulty, we started a new initiative in collaboration with another priest. We gathered hundreds of families and we divided them into groups for week-long stays. The summer camp will start at the beginning of June. Each week between 50 and 60 people will be welcomed in Slonfeh.

Everyone was afraid of leaving Aleppo. Nobody had even dared consider it because of the cost. So we decided to cover all costs: the journey, the meals, the accommodation, a priest to celebrate Mass and hold one spiritual meeting a day. We want people, including the elderly who in some cases have not left their homes for years, to be able to enjoy some peace and quiet, rest, songs and evenings together at last.

Courses and other pastoral activities

Pastoral activities and various assistance projects continue in the parish. During Lent, we prepared 24 young people for confirmation and after that, 10 children had their first communion after they completed the preparations. We then started the course for engaged couples. This year we have seven couples and during their meetings the large family of the church grows. They get to know one another, they listen to each other, they begin to feel responsible for each other. If a couple does not turn up, the others ask: "What's happened to them? We miss them." It is a family atmosphere that is growing and producing fruits.

There are also many engaged couples of other rites who come asking for our help. We always provide confidential support to engaged couples who need material help. Families today cannot afford to pay for the marriage of their children. When the couple is really mature and willing to take this courageous and counter-cultural step – the decision to choose consecration to God through family life – we support them.

We have met girls who even a week before their wedding did not have the money for their dowry, young people who had a job but still needed support, couples who had a house but still had to renovate or furnish it as well as others who had to find a solution by renting. We helped by covering the cost of renting an apartment for a year or repairing an empty house on condition that the owner was willing to leave it to a new family for a few years.

A family does not come into being by chance. It is always the result of many sacrifices, as we learned from our parents' example. Today in Aleppo, the family comes into being the same way, through a sacrifice offered by the whole Church; it is a project of the whole community.

The situation of the hospitals

So far, in this western part of the city, five hospitals have been bombed. One of them was very big and well-established. The paediatric Al-Quds hospital was also recently bombed. A missile killed 17 children. The eldest was only one year old. The media hardly mentioned it.

We live in the government-controlled part of the city and we do not know a lot about the other side, but unfortunately we know well what we and our people undergo every day.

Fortunately, a number of other hospitals and clinics are still working. For example, there are the private clinics run by nuns, such as the Sisters of St Joseph of the Apparition, who do invaluable work taking in all those injured by the bombings, Christians and Muslims alike. Thanks to close collaboration with these sisters we are able to help our people in various ways, which is very difficult after the departure of a large number of doctors. The sisters resisted the idea of closing the hospital and continued a life of sacrifice with great perseverance. We were witnesses of many miracles. There is really a very strong presence of our Lord in the middle of this city, which seems to be permanently at the mercy of war.

A living presence, in communion with the world

In conclusion, ours is a very strong and lively community. It bears a cross with very complex shades, but it is able to go beyond suffering and experience the force of the resurrection. This is certainly thanks to the aid we receive, with which we can give our life, time and breath. Without aid, however, it is not possible to carry on. The support, even minimal, from friends abroad with whom we are in profound communion is transformed into genuine miracles. Though they don't make the lame walk or restore sight to the blind, they are miracles of charity that have the power to totally change a situation, even with only a few euro.

28 MAY 2016[43]

The persecution of the Christians and the reaction of the Muslims

The war is considered a civil war, so it is not clear whether the jihadist groups' actions are motivated by anti-Christian sentiment. It is, however, undeniable that several times we as Christians have felt that we were the jihadists' specific target. In several cases, we have seen direct persecution. But it is not always visible and clear, nor is hatred always directed solely at Christians. The Muslims that live in our part of the city also feel persecuted by the fundamentalist groups that launch bombs and missiles against the areas where Christians and Muslims live together.

I remember one episode from five years ago, when the crisis began. Speaking to some Sunni Muslims, it was clear to me that they thought they were being persecuted. Afterwards some Shi'ites explicitly told me that they felt persecuted. Everyone perceived, with bitterness, that they were a target of the terrorists. As representatives of the Catholic Church, we arranged an official meeting with the Muslim leaders of Aleppo. The meeting was an extremely sincere and honest moment of friendship and sharing. On that occasion, one of our bishops said that we Christians were targeted by the jihadist groups. In reply, the leader of the Sunni Muslims said, "Observe, though, that the jihadist groups hate us more than they hate you Christians. They hate you because you belong to another religion, but we, who are Muslims, are considered heretics and this means that they hate us even more and intend to kill more of us than of you."

In conclusion, it is clear that Christians are being persecuted. It is just as clear that the jihadist groups direct their hostility towards everyone: Christians, Sunni and Shi'ite Muslims. Their missiles spare nobody.

The refusal to use violence

War is evil, without a doubt. Killing is always evil and violence is not a solution. Of people who choose to pick up weapons Jesus said: "All who

43 Meeting held at the parish of San Michele Arcangelo in Precotto, Milan

draw the sword will die by the sword" (Mt 26:52). The Catechism of the Catholic Church refers to the right to defend oneself under certain conditions. These conditions are unlikely to all be present at the same time. This undoubtedly applies to that part of the city which has always been governed by Bashar al-Assad and where the regular army is present. Many Christians have enrolled in this army, serve their country and exert their right of defence. Several young people enrolled before the crisis and are today forced to take up arms to perform their compulsory military service.[44] Is this fair? Those who lived in Aleppo five years ago and still live here believe that this is a legitimate choice, because it is linked to the need to defend their lives. In my opinion, however, this decision is not the best one. When Christians reason with weapons and war, justifying it with the urgency of defending themselves, the result is totally negative. One need only think of the experience of the Lebanese Christians during their civil war. Their case is for us, the Syrian church, a fundamental example.

We did not want to take up arms in the past and as a religious group we do not intend to take them up now. We have always firmly rejected this path. On several occasions, the government has officially asked us to form a Christian militia and the leaders of the church have refused this invitation every time. This is not to say that in Syria there are no Christians who have chosen to defend themselves with weapons, even outside the army.

The case of Sednaya and Kfarbo

In Syria there are two villages, Sednaya and Kfarbo, in which Christians have taken up arms to defend themselves from ISIS. Sednaya is in a strategic position on the road between Damascus and Homs. It is an inward-looking village with a Christian Syrian Orthodox majority, where everybody knows everybody else. It is distinguished by a strong and combative mountain mentality. In the face of the advance of ISIS from the mountains in 2015, the Christians bought weapons, positioned

44 In Syria, military service is compulsory for young men over 18. The period of conscription lasts 18 months. For women, military service is on a voluntary basis. Deserters risk life imprisonment or even the death sentence.

video cameras for the night, put up gates and small walls at various points and fought for several days. All the men and youngsters did guard duty day and night and defended their village from ISIS. The same happened in Kfarbo, another village in central Syria.

The situation, however, is very different in large cities such as Damascus or Aleppo where Christians have always lived in close contact with the Sunnis, Shi'ites, Kurds and Druze. In this type of situation, it is very difficult to hypothesise a defence with armed troops from the Christian quarters. It was therefore very courageous of the church to refuse the invitation to defend itself with weapons. This opposition also avoided the possibility of giving the impression that the Christians intended to defend themselves only.

A complex situation

For us, the regular army remains the fundamental point of the defence of the country and the Christians who are enrolled to defend it legitimately carry out this service. There is also, on the other hand, a current of Christians who ask: "What do we have to do with this war? We don't want to do military service." These young men leave Syria, meaning that the number of young males decreases considerably. For every boy in Aleppo today, there are about 11 or 12 girls.

In a nutshell, the situation is very complex. The war has created a great imbalance. If Christians were to flee, this would prevent us from stating to everyone that Syria is our country and that we want to defend it, together with all the other Syrians. It is not right that Shi'ites, Sunnis, Kurds should die in the military and we Christians voluntarily exclude ourselves from this war, maintaining that it has nothing to do with us. It is also our war, and someone has to defend the whole of Syria from ISIS.

Respect of the individual conscience

In every case, we have to recognise that a person has the right to refuse to take up arms and consider the possibility of replacing military service with civil service. We cannot, unfortunately, make the Assad government understand that the conscience of every single individual has to be respected. While on one side there are young people who feel up to carrying arms and fighting, on the other there are young people who, although trained, will not use weapons because of reasons of conscience. The government therefore ought to select people and be more flexible, offering the possibility of not taking up weapons to those who, for reasons of conscience, do not intend to fight.

The action of the Spirit and the spiritual instinct

Those who live every day with the Lord grow in communion with him and become a single being with our Father. As Paul writes: "I no longer live, but Christ lives in me" (Gal 2:20). There is no need for an intellectual quest to reach the decision to belong to him. The decision is triggered in man by something that has the strength of an instinct. This has been my experience. This does not mean that this is the only way for the Holy Spirit to move the decision of man. He also uses the path of intellectual reflection. What I experience, however, is a spontaneous path. When I faced decisions in the past and when I face them today, a sort of spiritual instinct takes over. There is something natural and strong, which does not require many words to be explained. It is like when a mother starts to look after her baby without having learned how to do it in the past; she pays attention to many details with all the love of a mother. It is the same instinct of the baby who places its mouth on her breast and, in a completely natural way, starts to drink.

I continue to experience this dynamic of instinctive charity, linked to our Christian nature. When we are granted perseverance by the Lord, this spiritual instinct of charity lives inside us, making us act in ways that are greater than what we are normally capable of and accomplish things that we would never even have dreamt of doing.

We priests carry within us this maternal instinct. St Gregory the Great cited a "fatherhood and motherhood of the priesthood", a natural instinct to help those who suffer. It makes us capable of helping and of listening to what the Holy Spirit asks us. Personally, I feel this energy of the Spirit in the choices, often challenging, that I continue to make every day; it is an energy that moves me in a spiritually instinctive way.

The steps towards charity

When Oriental spirituality refers to pure prayer and the passages that lead to the highest levels of prayer, it specifies that the first step is praying with the senses, that is, with the lips: raising your voice and pronouncing the prayers. Then you try to make the prayer reach the intellect. In this way, the prayer goes from a feeling to a thought. Then you reach the third passage, that of perfect prayer: the content descends from the intellect to the heart and you pray with the heart.

Many people have learned this when they started to pray, continuing it afterwards as well. Once it has been learned, they keep to this path. Those who traverse this path know when on a given day they may have prayed only with their lips. So they have to put more effort into it to think of the words that come out of their mouth and then to pray with the heart, which requires a greater effort.

The same thing happens with the steps that lead to charity. For example, I meet a stranger. I do not know him and I have been brought up throughout my childhood to make judgements and fit people into categories. So I observe him and make judgements, based first of all on physical criteria. The phases of prayer apply here as well. Even though I have to make a bit of an effort, I command myself to smile and I do it although I do not feel a drive to be charitable. Maybe I can even crack a joke to show that I am close to this person. They are very simple acts, but significant ones; they do not represent perfect charity, but nor are they attitudes of little importance. Then a further passage is made. After offering physical charity, the concrete signs of friendship and understanding, I start to worry about the other person, his situation, his suffering. I can see that he limps. Perhaps he has slept all night outside in the cold, without even a blanket. In this way I begin to implement the criteria of solidarity and respect for the mystery of the man who suffers.

Afterwards, slowly, with an even greater effort, I make the second passage and can succeed in looking at the stranger like the Good Samaritan looked at the man abandoned on the road between life and death. I succeed in seeing with compassion: "When he saw him, he took pity on him" (Lk 10:33). I identify with the situation of that man, I interpret his drama, I can feel his suffering as though it were mine. From here, the third passage of charity is reached. It is often simple. You have to get used to charity. When I make the effort to approach a person, when I am used to seeing people as Christ looks at them, charity becomes more spontaneous and immediate.

Sometimes, in front of another person, I feel that I have to take the first steps with the tongue, the next with the intellect, and the last with my heart. However, if I make the effort to love strangers more frequently, the same happens as with muscles: once they are trained, they become more agile, stronger and more resistant. It is the same with the spiritual battle of charity.

In conclusion, I know the truth; the path and the destination are clear to me. It is then that I have to make the effort to arrive, but this effort is often illuminated by grace.

When I pray and I approach the communion of the body and the blood of Christ, when I am more united with him, the Holy Spirit moves something in me and it becomes simpler to love everyone with the heart, to forgive, to be ready to give my life for those I do not know and to surprise myself by praying for those who persecute us.

The difficult path of the Christian

We Christians have to set off on the path of charity, improving ourselves all the time. We must not be discouraged when charity does not arise spontaneously. This does not mean that we are not real Christians. We are real Christians if we make the effort. Let us start out on the spiritual battle, let us train our charity, let us make an effort to love, always asking for the grace of our Lord and remembering that, without him, we can do nothing. Let's try to raise ourselves to pure charity, with the awareness that alone we cannot love. We always need grace.

The importance of looking at reality positively

I have noticed a slight pessimism among the Christians of the west, looking negatively in part at the Church, deeming it in difficulty. It is an attitude that I do not understand. Coming from Aleppo and spending a few weeks in Italy, I meet marvellous communities and many people who live the beauty of the Christian experience and communicate it with great certainty.

The same negative judgement is extended, not infrequently, to the field of politics. When, for example, there is talk of sanctions and the embargo which the European Union has placed on Syria since 2011, it is evident that these sanctions are unfair. It is concluded that the west cannot help suffering Syria and that, in fact, the west contributes to worsening the situation even more. In the west, they would like to do so much to help the Syrian people, but they are blocked because of the embargo. The conclusion is that, in the west, there is no mercy. In these cases in general, I answer that there are errors at a political level, but that the positive aspects cannot be denied.

I have met great solidarity in the west. When there is an appeal for the suffering church of Aleppo, everybody is mobilised. When the Pope proposed a world day of fasting and prayer for Syria (the last one was on 10 February) the whole Christian world takes action. Even the attitude of the various presidents and of the most powerful countries has changed.

Us Christians, in any case, are not allowed to judge reality pessimistically, because a view that is always negative can lead to despair and become injustice towards the Holy Spirit. In conclusion, we have to recognise the very many positive elements that inhabit reality and be able to promote and give thanks for the works which are the result of the Holy Spirit, who works and does great things in us.

"Here I am!"

The phase of life that took me from Rome to Aleppo is very interesting. I was studying, I had the material and plan ready for my PhD thesis, but suddenly the call came to go to Syria.

Father Pierbattista Pizzaballa, who was Custos of the Holy land at that time, had made an appointment with us and wanted to meet us individually. Getting ready for this meeting, I told myself that I would ask him if I could finish my PhD, which I had put off for too long. I would specify that only after the PhD would I be available for service. Once in front of the Father Custos, I saw that he was very tired and engrossed in his worries. I wanted to comfort and console him, so I said: "What is happening? I am ready to do whatever you say." As I said those words, I realised that I had not ordered my voice to say them. But the words echoed: "We are ready for everything and we are even willing to die."

The Custos explained that friars were needed in Syria. While my reason told me not to accept the post, my voice announced that I was ready. He was surprised. He could not believe me. He kept asking me if I really was willing to go. I answered again: "I am ready to go to Syria. You say the people are in need, so I feel ready." The Custos did not tell me where in Syria I was destined to go.

After a little while, Father Pizzaballa called me again. This is the method of obedience, which is shared obedience; the decision is reached slowly, it is reached together. The superior general asks for your opinion, if you feel up to the task. The Custos explained to me that friars were needed in Aleppo and once again asked me what I thought. At that point, the same answer I gave our Lord many years ago when I was 19 years old, came out of my mouth: "Here I am!"

I have had this experience several times in my life and I continue to have it. I often discover in myself the strength of the Holy Spirit, and it is this strength that lead me when I decided to give myself to our Lord. When God knows that your heart is willing to obey, you are kidnapped, even moved from one place to another, because he is certain that he really has the authority over your heart and your life.

After that first meeting with the Custos, I was disturbed. But I understood immediately that the Holy Spirit was sure of my readiness. The Spirit knows that I do not want to be the one guiding my life. I studied medicine for three years and it was a subject I loved very much, but I gave it up to enter the monastery because I did not doubt that by following our Lord I would be more gratified as a man than I could be by being a doctor. I will continue to give everything up. Our Lord knows that he can use my whole life in the way he wishes.

The harsh reality of Aleppo

After the last talks with my superiors, I went to visit Aleppo for three days together with the regional friar. My brothers feared that I might be shocked, but, from the psychological point of view, I was not disturbed in the face of fear, death or the bombs that were falling on us. What supported me was the fact that I had gone there with great joy.

Many people in Italy reproached me for this decision. I too have at times blamed myself for following my spiritual instinct. People in Aleppo were also surprised. Several parishioners asked me where I came from and, when I replied, they were amazed that I could have left Rome for Syria. Then I explained: "You think you are not worth much, that you are not important, but you are very precious and dear to our Lord. Many friars and bishops are ready to die for only one of you, as am I."

The Lord guides the will of men, freeing the heart

My will, I am certain, is not dead. It never dies, just as Jesus in the Garden of Gethsemane had a human will and human fear that resisted the idea of giving himself up. But on the other hand is the clear will of the Lord. In the case of Jesus, human will was always guided by that of the Father. The story of my departure for Aleppo, together with many other episodes in my life, consoles me because it shows me that I have a will of my own but what wins me over and comes out of my heart is what the Lord wants for me personally.

I do not hide that I went through a moment of crisis. There is a lot of talk about a crisis of priests but I say that a priest who goes through a moment of difficulty is fully human. After I was asked to go to Aleppo and went, I had to cope with a vocational crisis. But this was not a problem for me. I continued to enjoy the fact that divine will took complete possession of me, making me a collaborator of salvation.

On several occasions, I am aware that I have become capable of helping people in Aleppo, especially families. Never, for example, would I have thought that I would have distributed monthly food parcels, because this operation requires a lot of time and effort. I thought it was better to distribute money to families. One day, a phone call came and I was told, "We consider it is useful to give food parcels. Can you distribute 600 parcels to your people?" Without understanding, I immediately said yes. But once I put down the phone, I said to myself: "But I was against that and I still am!" The Lord however immediately superimposed his will on mine and that made me happy.

I have often meditated on the Acts of the Apostles, and in particular on the figure of Philip when he was taken away by the Lord. I said to myself: "Is it possible that God abducts a person, moves them from one place to another and makes them do something without their will? No, it is not possible, because God respects the will of man. So why should he have done that with Philip? Only because he was certain that Philip was wholly his."[45] The Spirit leads our steps, often with incredible gestures, and I am pleased about this.

Identifying with the will of God to become an instrument of good

A fact that occurred made me reflect on entrusting oneself to God. A few days ago, I was in Beirut in Lebanon. On the morning of my flight, I woke up at around 4am. In general, I do not have sleeping problems, but that day I woke up with only one thought: a young fiancé had wanted to speak to me. I had promised to call him but, because of the preparations for my journey, I had forgotten.

I recited a prayer for him then I sent him a message. I told him that I had not forgotten him and that we could talk by phone. I also told him not to worry, because a solution would be found for everything. I was almost certain that he had a problem, lack of money or a difficulty that would not have allowed him to get married on the scheduled date. I sent the message thinking that he would read it in the morning, but he replied immediately: "Father, I am pleased about your message. I cannot sleep because of worry; I have been awake all night. I am very anxious." I wrote to him again: "My dear boy, do not worry: everything will go for the best. We are with you. You are strong, try to remain calm. Pray, then we will see how the Lord solves every problem."

Even this simple message made me happier, because it is good to feel that the Lord possesses us completely. It is a consolation to realise

---

45 "And he gave orders to stop the chariot. Then both Philip and the eunuch went down into the water and Philip baptised him. When they came up out of the water, the Spirit of the Lord suddenly took Philip away, and the eunuch did not see him again, but went on his way rejoicing. Philip, however, appeared at Azotus and travelled about, preaching the gospel in all the towns until he reached Caesarea." (Acts 8:38-40)

that the Holy Spirit guides us, even when we wake up in the middle of the night to console someone or to give a word of comfort. For a priest, but also for a layman, there is nothing more comforting than to realise that it is the will of the Lord that guides our lives, making us men. Our will becomes his and we are taken towards the good destiny that God has prepared for us.

29 MAY 2016[46]

Today is a special day because, in Aleppo, the summer camp begins in our parish. Last year, 200 children took part four times a week, from the morning until after lunch. They shared a moment of joy together and with us. Although the missiles keep falling on our heads this year, we have organised the summer camp for two months.

Our children are full of fear of the bombs. This year they have also faced many difficulties in taking the end-of-year exams. There is a shortage of everything and with the collapse of the Syrian pound prices are going up, especially for food. There is no aid for the neediest families. 90 per cent of our families live below the poverty line. We friars distribute monthly food parcels. We have recently added vouchers to buy a small amount of meat. This gesture was welcomed with great joy.

Most of Aleppo's inhabitants have lost their jobs, so families can no longer support themselves. The result is a serious lack of security. two days ago, the Christian part of Aleppo was bombed all night long and the families in it were unable to sleep. Many ran out of their houses and slept in the streets. There were many dead and wounded, including children and young people.

We are going through a very particular situation. What makes it even more difficult is the absurdity of it all, not being able to understand the reason. This is why, driven by the Holy Spirit, this year again we wanted our children not to stay at home after school, worrying about the missiles. We wanted to get them out of isolation and take them to a place full of love and sharing, where they could get what their parents were

46 Homily delivered on the feast of Corpus Domini in the church of Santa Maria Assunta in Turro, Milan

unable to give them: a hot meal with meat and milk, a pair of trousers and shoes. All this is like a dream for them.

Last night, I learned that 270 children had enrolled. This is an encouraging sign for frightened parents as well, a sign of the breath of the Holy Spirit who pulls these small children into the church of the Father to share daily bread and eucharistic bread. It is an immense joy for us to see how the Lord continues to multiply his gifts, despite all the difficulties. God supports us and we feel deeply loved and cared for. We feel that we are in the arms of a tender, merciful and provident father. We experience this in many ways, including miracles.

One of these instruments of love is the numerous people, in particular young people from abroad, who have testified the contagious force of Christian charity by making room in their lives for those who are poor and suffering. We have never felt left alone. Last year, and this year again, our young people can feel loved by Jesus Christ, not only spiritually in the sacraments, but also materially, through what was offered to them thanks to the work of our many friends abroad.

In Aleppo, thanks to all those who have prayed for us and to their closeness, we have learned the fundamental lesson of Christian charity: "Greater love has no one than this: to lay down one's life for one's friends" (Jn 15:13). We Christians do not have another path; there is nothing finer than giving our life for our brothers. The school of charity is the life of Jesus.

30 MAY 2016[47]

The situation in Aleppo continues to be dramatic. The jihadist groups continue to strike indiscriminately. The population flee from many bombed parts of the city; about two-thirds have gone. Life is also very expensive, with the value of the Syrian pound continuing to fall.

Obstacles to sending aid

Caritas, unfortunately, is currently coming up against many obstacles to getting money to Syria. This institution, which should be the operative

47 Delivered at the parish of Gesù Divin Lavoratore, Milan

arm of the Catholic Church, is at present in great difficulty because every time the economic contributions to help the Syrian people arrive in Lebanon, they are sent back because of the embargo. As a consequence, Caritas, which used to support thousands of Christian families, has had to reduce the number of families it helps and the number of projects it undertakes.

It is a great problem we also face. When, for example, a private individual has wanted to send us a large sum of money, he has had to go several times to the bank to explain that it was money for our parish. Nonetheless, we never received these funds.

The same difficulties apply to many parish priests, especially Americans, who would like to help us but cannot because the banks prevent them. People who left Syria and want to send aid to their people are faced with so many complications that in the end they too are forced to give up.

Peaceful coexistence before the war and the subsequent changes

In Aleppo, there is a religious plurality which has always been distinguished by peaceful coexistence and mutual respect. The majority of the population are Sunni Muslims and, for a very long time, the Christians have lived in peace with them. There are also Shi'ites, Kurds and Druze. As Christians, our religious freedom has always been respected. We could profess our faith publicly, for example, in Easter processions and those at the end of the Marian month. Our rights were recognised and we were able to express our testimony through schools and even sports associations. We lived in peace and in mutual aid, even though there were betrayals by Muslims who handed Christians over to jihadist groups to ask for ransoms.

We live in the western part of the city, which is still in the hands of the regular army, with both Sunni and Shi'ite Muslims. We live together in peace. Suffering has united us, making us more sincere and direct in our relations. We help each other more, sharing needs and solutions. There are Muslims who have welcomed Christians who lost everything in the bombing into their homes. Christians did the same for Muslims. Muslims are often seen taking part in the prayer for the dead at Christian funerals. The same applies to weddings. There are Christians who go to Muslim weddings and Muslims who go to Christian weddings.

So what has changed? The change has taken place in the Muslim world and has got to do with the division between the Sunnis and the Shi'ites. A long time ago, we started to see some intellectual differences between them, but these were of little importance. We never could have imagined these differences would explode into such a violent war. Unfortunately, blood has divided the two communities. There are conflicting interests and not even a glimmer of hope can be seen for a positive solution of the crisis. It thus becomes difficult to think of a future in which there can once again be peaceful coexistence among Muslims. This is a great danger for us Christians; as long as there is a conflict between Muslims, it seems impossible to think of a future when we can once again live in peace.

There is also a strong desire for revenge among the population. A Sunni driver who took me to Aleppo told me: "We know who is launching the missiles, we know them by name. Even if the regular army were to implement a truce and there were to be a reconciliation, we would continue fighting until the bitter end, until we have killed them all."

War broke out in a world where there had been coexistence. The real problem is the clear-cut division in the Muslim world and the accentuation of this division, which makes the scenario increasingly difficult. It is a conflict that risks never coming to an end.

An ecumenism of blood

In Aleppo we are experiencing a real ecumenism of blood. Many times, after a missile has fallen Catholics and Orthodox pray together in the streets. We have spent whole afternoons together after these prayers. Even before the war, our city was special from this point of view. This ecumenism was already present. For some time, the bishops (not only the Catholic and Orthodox bishops, but also the leaders of the Protestant churches) met three times a year to discuss the problems of the churches and society. For years, there have also been personal meetings between priests of the different faiths. Before, it was very rare that we asked one another for help. Now, on the other hand, everyone makes room for the others in their community.

When we opened the holy door in our church, everyone came.[48] The same happens in front of difficulties; everyone feels the need to invoke God's intervention. So without even organising it we sometimes meet together to pray, as happened on 13 May.[49] Praying with all the Christians in church on that day, we decided to make an act of consecration to the immaculate heart of Mary. This ecumenism is therefore precious and it has become stronger than ever. In two years, difficulties have been dispelled and we have moved towards an ever deeper communion.

The importance of the respect for religious pluralism

In Syria, if a Christian man married to a Christian woman becomes Muslim, the children under 18 are declared Muslim and have to study Islam. Only when they are 18 can they choose whether to remain Muslim or go back to being Christians. The same happens for mixed marriages: if the Muslim spouse dies, the son is not entrusted to the Christian parent unless they officially become Muslim. This represents a problem for us. The Christian parent cannot receive any inheritance either.

These are the practical obstacles posed by a state law which is, in certain respects, ambiguous. As Christians, we do not demand that others observe a social law prepared by us; we do not want to put others in the difficulty in which we are today. We have no problems accepting a lay law. Indeed, we are pleased to when laity is understood in a positive sense and not as hostile to Christianity. In dialogue, we start from the concept of the lay state and from there we slowly build up a society in which everyone has the right to be themselves. Our strength is in dialogue. We uphold the principles of common good and solidarity, as well as a social doctrine based on the respect for every identity.

In short, we believe it is important for every religion to contribute to the growth of the country and respect pluralism, which is a fundamental factor of society.

....

48 C.f. p.43
49 C.f. p.159

Forgiveness as freedom from the slavery of sin

We have to ask for forgiveness and be able to forgive in the most diffi-cult of times. People in Aleppo have always obeyed when I asked them to forgive and this surprised me greatly. I asked them to pray for those who kill us and people listened, even – and this is definitely not to be taken for granted – parents whose son had been killed. They prayed with us for his assassins. Here we can see the work of the Holy Spirit and a great maturity of faith.

In the gospels, Jesus spoke of forgiveness several times. On the cross, he asked his Father to forgive those who had put him to death, though they didn't ask for forgiveness. In the same way, in the Acts of the Apostles, while the assassins of Stephen were stoning him, the martyr had the strength to kneel and, like Jesus, invoke forgiveness for those who were killing him (Acts 7:55-60).

I personally consider what is happening in my community to be a victory of the resurrection: the victory of charity over hatred. Some-times, during the sacrament of reconciliation, someone confesses feel-ings of hatred for our enemies. I ask them to forgive and each time the person is willing to do this. There is no finer experience than this. It shows a freedom of the heart from the slavery of sin and I am deeply grateful to our Lord for the fact that the faithful can forgive.

Bearing witness to Christ, until martyrdom

The term martyr means witness: someone who witnesses to the truth to the point of giving one's life. In Syria, people are very worried about bread and water. In such a context, how can we bear witness to Christ? Since arriving here, I have tried to explain to my parishioners that Chris-tians must not be primarily concerned with eating and drinking, or the danger of missiles. The priority is how to assert their faith, carrying the cross in front of others. I have tried to speak with freedom of this task and I was moved to see that people immediately followed me.

Christians in Aleppo know that they are in the midst of bombs and rubble to bear witness to beauty and a truth which is greater than the dramatic situation in which they are plunged. They are obviously very worried about their ordinary needs. But they know that even when drawing water they must show peace of heart, the peace that comes from Christ. This is our faith, if we want to be faithful to Christ's message.

If we think of our lives in terms of giving witness, then reaching martyrdom is almost taken for granted. In Aleppo, Christian communities are asking dramatic and essential questions: "If ISIS arrives, Father, how must we bear witness to Christ?" We have to be ready to hand over our lives at any time. We must be up to the testimony that Jesus gives us with his presence that never abandons us.

31 MAY 2016[50]

Today in Syria, there are conflicting interests. The economic one is very significant because there are many oil and gas wells. Linked to this is the geographical position of Syria; it is strategic for transporting gas. This is the source of disagreement between different countries. Then there is the religious element, which from my point of view is secondary. The primary interest is the economic aspect, linked to the drive for domination and power. Who will control the whole of the Middle East?

At the moment, it is the lack of an international agreement that is blocking peace. As Pope Francis has maintained for several years now, a world war is raging in pieces, a war which also involves the Middle East. It is more than a civil war. So, to reach peace an agreement has to be reached and this is what is missing today. In the analysis of the current situation, however, we have to start from the division of Syrian territory.

The Syrian territory: geography, resources, role of foreign powers

The surface area of Syria is about 183,000km²; its coast along the Mediterranean is 160km long. The country has borders with Turkey in the north, Iraq in the east and south-east, Jordan in the south, Lebanon in the west and Israel in the south-west.

Before this conflict, Syria was already divided in certain ways. The capital Damascus and other important cities are in the south. Syria's second city, Aleppo, is in the north, only 70km from the Turkish border.

....

50 Delivered during a prayer meeting in the sanctuary of the Santissima Trinità Misericordia in Maccio di Villa Guardia, Como

Before the war Aleppo had hundreds of industrial companies controlling the trade of the area, not only of Syria, but also of Turkey.[51] There are other important cities. Tartus, on the south coast, is Syria's second-largest port and since 1971 has been the site of a Russian naval base. From the time of the Cold War, this city has been considered the only window of Russia on the Mediterranean and it therefore plays a very important role from a strategic point of view. However, it is not only Tartus that is under the control of the Russians, but also a good part of the west.

All the forces of ISIS are in the north-eastern part of Syria, as well as in other areas. There are also many groups and militias of jihadists who sometimes fight the regular army, but more often fight each other.

There are also groups of Kurds. Kobane, for example, is a city already marked by fighting between Kurds and ISIS. Its borders were the point of passage of armed jihadist groups, trained and prepared to carry out war in the streets. Their main border of passage is that with Turkey, where there is a strip of territory that allows this access.

Syria's wealth is mainly in the north-east of the country, with oil wells and enormous wealth near the Mediterranean coast also. The Russians, as mentioned above, are there trying to make this wealth theirs, while the US, in different ways, is trying to claim the north-east.

At the moment, Turkey is not satisfied because it has its sights on Aleppo. The destruction of 110 industrial companies at the start of the crisis was not enough for Turkey; it aspires to take possession of a large strip in the north, rich in water, olive trees, cotton and other resources.

In summary, today Syria is divided into parts: we have Russia, while to the west is the regular army and to the north-east is the presence of the Kurds and of ISIS.

From my point of view, there are many countries interested in wiping out Syria and the interests driving the continuation of this war are more numerous than those seeking peace. Without a doubt, many billions have been spent to keep this conflict going.

Aleppo in the line of fire

Aleppo is currently in the eye of the cyclone. It has a very large periph-

51 C.f. p.178

eral area, the largest of all Syrian cities, which goes right up to the Turkish border. Unlike Damascus, which is almost completely under the control of the regular army, and Latakia and Tartus, which have the presence of the Russians and the force of the regular army, Aleppo is still in the line of fire because it is divided. All the groups want to enter Aleppo at all costs. Turkey, as anticipated, aims to exercise its influence over the city, while the regular army is defending it.

Aleppo is currently divided into two: the eastern part is controlled by ISIS, while the western part, where all the Christian communities live, is still under the control of the regular army. Effectively though, this area is surrounded by jihadist military groups, which continually launch missiles on the population. The Christian community that still lives in the western part comprises 12,000 families, belonging to all the different rites: Latin, Oriental and Orthodox. However, we do not know exactly how many citizens there are in the western part or in the eastern part because there is a border between them.

The scenarios facing us are reminiscent of the Second World War: destruction and rubble that change the face of the city every day. Every time we hear a missile fall, we start to run towards where it fell to be able to help the people, pray with them and offer emergency services. Many parts of the city are in this situation.

The churches are destroyed

More than 60 per cent of the churches in Aleppo have been destroyed. When I see the ruined churches, I remember the catacombs where the first Christians prayed. Here the Christians do not have a place of worship. Some sought refuge in the cathedral of the Maronites, which has now been gradually damaged until the whole roof collapsed. The area around the cathedral was the most prestigious in Aleppo, but now this area is in the sights of the jihadists. There is nobody there any more; all the inhabitants have fled. The bishop, who did not want to abandon his beautiful church, would go there every day and in the evening would come and stay with us. Now, since it is dangerous even to go there for a walk, he and another priest have sought refuge in our monastery. After the last missiles were launched, he did not have the strength to go back.

As far as St Francis of Assisi is concerned, all the tiles on the roof are still shattered because we have not been able to repair anything. We are waiting for better times to be able to start the work. At the same time, the holy door opened for the jubilee on 12 December 2015 remains wide open while all the other doors of the church are closed.

To mention a last example of devastation close to us: one day a missile fell in the square behind our church, leaving three cars burnt out and destroying several houses. On that occasion, I went with blessed water to pray with the people and keep them company in that dramatic and surreal scenario. Our intervention was supported by economic aid, as well as by the operations of rescue teams.

Hoping against all hope

It is now clear that this conflict cannot be solved by arms or through diplomacy. Chaos reigns and no solution can be found. This is why we are desperate, because there does not seem to be any way out. But we hope against all hope. We know that anything that has a start in history at a certain point will come to an end. The hope that the risen Lord can draw good from evil remains alive in us more than ever.

1 JUNE 2016[52]

The elements at play; the root of the crisis

There are many elements influencing the reality of this conflict in Syria today. On the one hand, the Russian presence based in the city of Tartus disturbs the other countries that wish to eliminate one of the last outposts of the former USSR outside Russian territory. On the other hand, there is the influence of the rest of the Muslim world. Though Saudi Arabia and Qatar are a certain distance away in the south, their influence is considerable and the dream of recreating the ancient caliphate to control the whole Islamic world is still alive. Iran, in the north-east, is the Shi'ite centre where the desire to lead all the Muslim countries has always been cultivated.

52 Meeting organised by the Massimiliano Kolbe Cultural Centre

Lastly, Turkey is also not far from manifesting similar ambitions: they too desire to occupy a certain centrality in the Muslim world. Israel in the south – small, surrounded by various larger Muslim countries and always feeling under attack – is also equipped to defend itself.

To top off these already very significant factors is the presence of oil and gas and the gas pipelines which come from Iran and Russia, passing through Syrian territory to serve the whole of Europe.

Today, after five years of war, there is talk of 300,000 dead, but it is only a symbolic figure because the number is far higher.

The project for the Middle East is a new plan: creative chaos, as it began to be called after 11 September 2001. The chaos implies the death of millions of people, but it is "creative" because it becomes possible to take advantage of the situation to change the international stakes, at all levels. These words have already been pronounced by several politicians in the past and their meaning has become clear to us only today.

The role of ISIS

The western part of Syria and a strip extending south to Damascus are now under the protection of the Russian military base of Tartus. ISIS is in the north-east, as are the Kurds led by the special troops and supported on the ground with soldiers from the United States.

ISIS is undoubtedly ambiguous, a monster that seems to have appeared out of nowhere. Almost 60,000 trained people descend upon oil wells and strategic positions with sophisticated arms and the ability to wage sophisticated warfare. Questions emerge which affect us all. Who created and trained this monster? Who gives it weapons? Who provides the data, the detailed logistic information to anticipate the moves of the regular army? Who anticipates the coordinates to launch missiles?

These groups are becoming richer by the day because they are selling oil which does the rounds of the whole international market. But who buys it then? This is also a question to be asked.

I conclude by saying that someone has created this monster and though it is being hunted by many countries nothing changes. Why are so many countries against this monster, but it remains alive?

Aleppo divided and contested

All the terrorist groups, including hundreds of jihadists and the Kurdish activists, are present in the huge outskirts of Aleppo. These groups often fight one another, but other times they form coalitions against different groups or against the government troops.

In the eastern part of the city there are various rebel groups labelled "moderate". We have only heard of this moderate position from the international media. We only see terrorists. Those who launch missiles against homes, terrifying the innocent population, and against schools or hospitals, killing children, cannot be part of a moderate rebellion. The Christian communities live in the western part of the city, surrounded by the various jihadist militias.

The city is suffering because of countless problems, the main one being the lack of water. We have tried to find various solutions to this problem. First, we offered the water from our well with the help of volunteers who distributed it for many hours of the day, often helping the elderly to carry it to their homes. Then we brought out vans with large tanks to which we connected pumps. A family calls to request assistance and the vans go to fill their stores with water. We can only meet this need partially, as it involves a huge number of households.

There is still no electricity and a lot concern over the lack of work. Damascus also suffers from this problem, but not like Aleppo. Here, only 20 per cent of the population has even partial employment, which is insufficient to provide for families but at least means that people do not stay at home unemployed.

The cost of living also continues to rise because many shopkeepers take advantage of the falling value of the Syrian pound by selling food such as vegetables at a very high price. When the government is weak, groups of dishonest people dominate and it is the poor people who are in difficulty.

In this already difficult scenario, missiles of up to 9m (29ft) strike, destroying buildings and homes. These instruments of death do not attack schools and hospitals casually: they are always targeted objectives. It is not by chance that they have hit children just after school or in the morning assembly before class. Something similar happened with the churches and mosques: every Holy Week, for instance, they were attacked. This year during Easter the jihadists hit many houses, killing a huge number of young people and children.

The western part of the city is now very small. The jihadists have all the coordinates, so they can target and hit exactly where they want. Because of these continuous and unforeseeable attacks, people are no longer able to reason; the terror drives them crazy. The city is destroyed, and the vast majority of the country is in a similar state.

Small, possible projects

In addition to larger aid projects like repairing houses, alleviating mortgage debt, distributing monthly food parcels and covering the cost of electricity, the church also carries out what we call "small, possible projects". Here is an example.

One day, the wife of an important entrepreneur, a former store-keeper who had various industrial properties and restaurants, came to see me. He lost facilities and machinery; everything was destroyed by bombs. All he had left was his house and he had almost paid off the mortgage. This mortgage had never been a problem due to his substantial resources but he was now threatened with being evicted from his home. He had a son who did not know what to do, because there was no work, and his wife had sold all the family's gold, even her wedding ring.

The woman explained their situation but I answered that their debt was greater than what we were used to dealing with. What's more, they did not have work. I asked her where her husband was and she told me that he was at home. He couldn't bring himself to come. Never in his life had he asked anyone for money because he had been very rich. His wife added that he also suffered from heart problems. I invited him to the office for a coffee. We talked about what he thought of doing, then I told him: "We can only pay off part of your debt. Let's try and create an opportunity for you and your son to work. I'm sure you know your way around the world of work. What do you think? Any ideas?" He answered: "We can rent a shop for a year and sell what we can, maybe even with your help. We can do something!" I accepted because I was expecting something similar. Saying goodbye, the man then said: "Tonight I can at last sleep a little. After so many sleepless nights, I will be able to rest."

In the end, that man rented a sandwich shop. His wife prepares them and sells them with her son and now, despite numerous sacrifices, their condition has improved and they can at least meet the monthly mortgage repayments for their house.

This is why talk about small, possible projects. They are initiatives through which young people or men who have lost capital can begin again and not remain unemployed until they fall into despair. In this way, we have helped a number of young people who had lost their jobs but were serious, creative and with a great desire to work. At the moment, for example, we are helping a couple who have each opened a shop and can now get married.

Entrusting the future to the Lord only

Two years ago, we started from nothing in terms of aid management. I remember I found spending even 100 euro very hard at first; I was uncertain about whether to do it or not. I worried that I might spend and then receive no help or donations in the following days. Once we stopped using a calculator, gave ourselves up to charity, stopped thinking about the future and left it to the Lord, everything started going well. I don't know how. Often, when our monthly statement shows the large amount spent on charity, I wonder: "Did we really spend that much? Where did we get all that money?" It is certainly the work of Providence.

We know nothing about the future. We do not know why we, unlike others, have been spared. We help families and people not to despair so that, free from terror and despair, they might choose their future.

The responsibility of testimony

After our church of St Francis was hit several times as I celebrated Mass, I often said to myself: "Lord, I entrust my spirit into your hands. Love all these people's spirits too." Though the jihadists now have the coordinates and could kill us at any moment, we feel that behind all this there is a mission, an important responsibility that God is entrusting to us.

Now, after only two years, we no longer feel up to opening our doors because we do not have the resources. We left this task to Caritas, but then it encountered obstacles.[53] We are here and we are responsible not only for the Christian community but also for witnessing to the Muslim community, to the many people who are suffering.

We do not want to save ourselves. I am not worried about dying tomorrow. I am ready to accept it. When I agreed to go to Aleppo, I knew perfectly well what I would encounter. I am very afraid of the idea of not being available to give everything that I have to the people who come knocking on our door.

I like to think of us Christians as a weak plant which can easily be trodden on, but is never cut down and never dies, because our charity depends on the charity of Jesus and therefore overcomes death. The Kingdom of Heaven is already present in the hell of Aleppo.

11 JUNE 2016[54]

Dear brothers and sisters who are taking part tonight in the pilgrimage from Macerata to Loreto this year, may all peace and good be yours.

In Aleppo, we continue our via crucis. The burden of suffering is enormous. Every day we see corpses and wounded and mutilated people. We are faced with a very high number of houses that have been damaged and destroyed and there is deep despair and fear among the people. The threats from the military groups surrounding us continue.

After almost five years of war, we see general despair among the clergy of the various rites and the population. The situation was terrible and we could see no way out, either diplomatic or military. So, on 13 May we unanimously decided to once again consecrate Aleppo and the world to the immaculate heart of Mary. We all perceived this petition as very important at a time when we felt attacked and in danger of being killed. On 13 May all the community was present in the church of St Francis: bishops, vicars, priests, religious and many laypeople from the various Christian rites. There were also many Muslims, who came out of curiosity or out of faith to be present at this consecration.

53 C.f. p.146

54 Message from Aleppo for the 38th pilgrimage from Macerata to Loreto on foot

When we have no more weapons for fighting evil, when we feel evil prevail, we want to run like children into the tender embrace of Mary, who represents the tenderness and mercy of God. In this act of consecration, we asked her for the strength of faith, charity and hope, to be able always to continue our pilgrimage with and towards her son Jesus.

The natural relationship between a child and a mother is fundamental and we have all experienced it. Growing up with his mother, a child feels deeply loved and unique. In the same way we, as individuals and as a Christian community, have always felt unique before our celestial Mother, who looks after us, follows us, guides and defends us. This is what a child feels and it is what we also feel, even in Aleppo.

By consecrating the whole of Aleppo and the world to Mary again, we have also consecrated our hearts – where evil finds different ways to stay alive – to her again. We offer Mary the evil that surrounds us and threatens us. We asked her for the strength to be real witnesses of that tenderness of God that appeared in her as well. We want to answer evil with good, hatred with forgiveness, violence with peace. It is our path, which we take every day in Aleppo and which I think you too in Italy along with all Christians in different parts of the world continue to take.

I accompany you spiritually on this beautiful pilgrimage. I would have liked to have been there with you physically but it was not possible. So I propose that we really address our thought to Mary, that through this pilgrimage we once again consecrate ourselves to the immaculate heart of Mary. We want to feel more loved by her, cared for, guided on the path of good, accompanied in the struggle between good and evil.

We want good always to triumph in our lives. We also want to be the defenders of good in our societies and to be increasingly serious in our path as Christians. We want to take part in the mystery of Jesus Christ, his incarnation in the midst of people and his free gift of himself, without limits or conditions, to the whole of mankind.

Invocation to Mary
Mary, we entrust ourselves to you: allow good to win in us.
Mary, we entrust our families to you; allow them always
To be in the right place to grow in a holy life,

In wisdom and in grace, before God and men.
Mary, we entrust our societies, full of suffering, to you,
Full of searching for your Son.
The more this search is unconscious and indirect,
The more we offer you the world, which lives in an imbalance
Between avarice and the search for power and wealth.
We offer the whole world to you
and all of ourselves to you, Mother, so that
We can feel unique: not as a privilege, but to become
Responsible for the whole world.
We want all of us to grow in your hands and always succeed
In being operators for the construction and expansion
Of the Kingdom of our Father
United in prayer, in the pilgrimage, in the path
And in testimony.

9 AUGUST 2016[55]

"Father, into your hands I commit my spirit." This is the prayer we say every time we have to go out. As well as the bombings, the presence of snipers makes life more difficult. The bombing intensified during the night and there are still missiles falling here in the inhabited parts of western Aleppo. We know nothing about the situation of the war, but we feel its negative effects. Many people are frightened. There is no electricity and the water has been cut off again. Prices have shot up. In the past few days, two areas have been evacuated and many people are sleeping in the streets and in tents. I doubt that the conditions are being created for a truce: we expect the arrival in Aleppo of many soldiers and we do not see the calm that precedes a truce. The army wants to regain control of the areas it has lost in the past few days, while various military groups are getting ready to advance towards Hamadaniya and

55 In early August bombing by the jihadist militia intensified, while thousands of men from the Syrian army of Assad prepared for what the media called the "final battle" against the militia in control of the eastern part of the city, a battle which would last for months. From an interview with Luca Collodi (Reuters)

the west of Aleppo. I deliberately do not use the world rebels because at the moment, the situation we are living in makes it clear that it is the jihadists more than the rebels who are guiding all these extremely diversified groups of soldiers. It is a miracle and a gift of Divine Providence that were able to buy food before the main road in the city was closed. From tomorrow, we will be able to distribute the food parcels for this month to thousands of families. We do not know what will happen. We have announced to all the priests and people that we want to fast and pray in the next 72 hours, so that the will of peace defeats that of war.

20 AUGUST 2016[56]

Man is being destroyed here

We are facing the height of the crisis. For five years, we have been subjected to continuous waves of violence. This last one, though, is a wave of death, the worst ever seen. Families' spirits are suffering from fear of the bombings, illnesses, psychological traumas, the evil done to their children. Their bodies suffer due to great economic difficulties. There is a shortage of everything: water, electricity, medicines and food. There is no work to earn that small amount of bread necessary to survive. Today Aleppo is like the destroyed cities of the Second World War or of more recent times, such as Sarajevo. I do not think that violence like that which is destroying Syria has ever been seen.

This is what makes me bitter. Rebuilding roads, schools and buildings is always possible, but what about rebuilding the hearts of men? Not only of Christians, but of everyone who lives here, especially those who refuse to take up arms because they want to live in peace. Children suffer and the powerful continue trading the fate of our country. Today, bread is not enough; we need a solution, an end to this torture. The fault lies with those people or groups we call traders, or those enriched by the war. Those who guide the fate of the world and of different countries should not have this self-interested mentality: the risk is that man is deprived of his dignity and sold. We do not want the international

56 From an interview with Daniele Rocchi (SIR)

community to lower itself to this level. It seems like every power is applying pressure according to its own interests to solve a crisis that kills thousands every day. We hope that the international community can dialogue, thinking of the good of people, of every person.

Those who write history must have mercy for the devastated and suffering in Syria today, especially in Aleppo. Many of our faithful tell us that they see the finest face of the church, a mother church that worries about and spiritually and materially helps her children. I can say that the church of Aleppo is a radiant church, full of light, faith, hope and charity, not only for its children, but for the whole of the Syrian people. Our church is on its knees to wash the feet of the lepers of the twenty-first century: the poor, the weak, the refugees and the victims of conflicts.

9 SEPTEMBER 2016[57]

We are frightened. The two international lions (Russia and the US) cannot come to an agreement and so the truce does not exist. We are worried because this has taken the war into a very complicated phase. We friars have organised food parcels for all families and a parcel with detergents, soap and nappies. We would also like to concentrate on the future of the young people who are here. There are thousands of children who have to go to school, young people who would like to go to university and others who would like to get married and start a family. We need educational projects, but in order to develop them we would also need to time to work out a plan. Bombs and snipers slow everything down. Then there is the arrival of winter to think about; people will need diesel oil for heaters and prices are now sky-high.

My friar friends and I have asked ourselves many questions about the risk of people becoming dependent on the aid. The situation has been unbearable for years now and hundreds of families depend on our help to find work or money for medical care. It is like a mother who has an ill and weak child in need of care. Of course, the child must be corrected, educated and brought up by his parents, but his mother also knows that her child first needs to experience tenderness, to be protected and looked after. This

57 From an interview with Maria Acqua Simi (*Il Giornale del Popolo*)

is what we are doing now. There is the risk of dependence. The alternative is that without aid people will die or flee by sea. Without this intervention there would no longer be any Christians in Aleppo. I do not want my people to be spoilt, but I do not want them to die either.

We have many young people here: young widows, young couples who get married despite everything and, above all, many children, with lots of baptisms every year. This is also a small miracle in the middle of the war. This is why we continue to run a course for engaged couples, to help them take this great step in front of God. We are particularly fond of young people because they are the future of Aleppo. Many of them were born in the war and know nothing else. We would like to help them study. In our monastery we are now hosting the Sisters of the Holy Rosary, who used to have a beautiful school (currently occupied by the militia). The children are now studying in a somewhat makeshift school and we often let those who need light to do their homework or their after-school activities use our space. We would like to be able to improve on the work of Sister Giacinta and Sister Natalie. In our area, there are about 20 Christian schools of different rites, attended by Muslims as well. They should be reopening on 29 September and we would like to be able to help families pay the school fees as well as give a hand with the teachers' salaries, which are always too low. The Christian presence in the field of education has always been appreciated by our city, by everyone. It would be wonderful to be able to continue.

There is a high level of collaboration between the different Christian churches and I have to say that, thanks to the great help we have received this year, we have been able to support not only the Latin Catholic community, but also all the others. Since January, we have been able to support vast projects. Our task is to serve anyone who needs help, without reservations. Priests from the other Christian rites (including Orthodox) have often sent injured or needy people to our door and we have always answered it. They have sent us people who needed medical care and we sent the people to the hospital of the Sisters of St Joseph. We have supported them because their hospital is one of the few in which good doctors are still working.

The beautiful thing is that this condition of aid has generated a new life, which all revolves around the church. We do not only pay attention to material needs; the soul also has to be comforted and helped to mature. We must not think that because we are at war everything has to remain on stand-by. As Franciscan friars, our mission is also to help our people to keep and grow in faith. This is why we provide spiritual assistance with the sacraments: the courses for engaged couples, the catechism for children and adults. It is a challenge that is above all a reminder for us of the beauty of our task here.

14 SEPTEMBER 2016[58]

With the help of benefactors, we buy food and medicine and we distribute them to the people. We are not waiting for the arrival of humanitarian aid, because it is impossible to organise constant and regular monthly aid. The water shortage has improved slightly, although the water is still contaminated and undrinkable. Our greatest torment is the missiles falling on our heads, on homes and in the streets; people can no longer take it. Many, including many of our families, have decided to leave the country. Our second great torment is the general situation of the city; not having work means that families have no regular monthly income, so the number of poor and needy families continues to increase. This then leads to depression, to various psychological problems and to people becoming desperate.

My day runs from 8am to 11pm. There are people to see, problems to try to solve, meetings, visits. Another difficult task continues during the night: answering the messages and letters from our friends and benefactors. It is a very long and very tiring day. We have not had even half a day off for months and months. Our spiritual and pastoral service in itself already takes up a lot of time and we have also adopted humanitarian aid as a way of being with the people. We cannot drop that.

58 From the evening of 12 September 2016, a fragile ceasefire had been in place, following an agreement between the United States and Russia. People were waiting for humanitarian convoys to arrive. Government-controlled west Aleppo, where Father Ibrahim lives, still had many needs. From an interview with Emanuela Campanile (Vatican Radio)

Here in Aleppo, there are five Franciscan friars who help in the parish. We still have the consecrated around us: the Jesuits, the Salesians, various congregations of sisters who try to help. The centre, though, is always the parish. Hundreds and hundreds of families are part of the Latin rite; in the west of Aleppo there are about 40,000 of us. I have to say that many of them are elderly, abandoned, alone. There are lots of widows and lots of small children without a father or without a mother. A missile can fall at any time and then we have to intervene immediately, visit, pray with the people and be always beside those who suffer.

It is not only Christians who live here. Like before the crisis, there are people of all rites and all religions here. We have always lived like this and we will continue to live like this. There is great respect and great collaboration and we always try to stretch out our hand with humanitarian aid because it is our Lord Jesus Christ who always drives us on with the commandment to help others. We continue to give life as we saw our model Jesus Christ do. We continue to love, up to giving our life for our brothers.

24 September 2016[59]

We are living in great confusion and great instability. When international powers do not agree it has consequences for our daily life. In the past few nights, we have not been able to sleep because of the bombs and missiles and there have been dead and wounded. A young father was hit by a missile. He was taken to hospital and, thanks be to God, has been saved but bears on his body the signs of the violence. At this moment uncertainty, bitterness and fear for the future prevail.

The problem is the confusion between the so-called moderate sides and the so-called fundamentalist sides. On the one hand, the Russians

59 Aleppo continued to burn. The situation for inhabitants was worsening. At the United Nations, there was no concrete step to re-establish the truce mediated by the United States and Russia. Washington's John Kerry and Moscow's Serghei Lavrov nonetheless spoke of "small progress" in the talks aimed at "preserving" the "ceasefire" established on 19 September in Geneva, which effectively fell through. From an interview with Giada Aquilino (Vatican Radio)

and the regular army said that the truce had to be respected with regard to the moderate groups, while the bombings had to continue unceasingly against al-Nusra,[60] against al-Qaeda and against the so-called Islamic State. The ambiguity and the lack of collaboration between all the parties, including international forces and other foreign countries, are what is creating the most confusion.

The hope in my community is that these waves of evil, this stormy wind will not prevail. I am speaking not only in the name of the Christian community, but in the name of all religions and all the members of any group, all those who live here and are victims of this absurd war.

3 OCTOBER 2016[61]

This morning, in an area called Bintan, the bombings caused many houses to collapse on their inhabitants. Lots of people abandoned their houses to avoid violence and escape death. We are suffering from a lack of water. People keep knocking on the door of the monastery. Yesterday morning, Sunday, lots of people came to ask if we would be distributing drinking water. We continue our service as best we can. There is no electricity. There are no medicines; there are no drugs for cancer or other chronic diseases. People keep dying because they have no medical care. There is a shortage of doctors and of specialists; there are very few of them now and they cannot help everyone. two days ago, we met the UNICEF personnel who have reached this government-controlled part of the city. But apart from them, we have not seen any other international organisations. Médecins Sans Frontières are in the eastern part of the city, but not here with us. We have many people who are seriously wounded, including many children.

27 OCTOBER 2016[62]

There are no words that can describe the situation in Aleppo. We live, as a people, without electricity, often without water, without work, with

60 Al- Nusra is an armed group affiliated with al-Qaeda, active in Syria and Lebanon.
61 From an interview with Radio 24
62 From an interview with Marina Tomarro (Vatican Radio)

the rocketing food prices and with bombs, which fall on schools, hospitals, churches, mosques, homes and streets. We cannot see any way out and there is no military solution for Aleppo, though the parties intend to have it over and done with through military means.

The numbers of Christians are diminishing. The scourge of emigration affects all the population, minorities in particular, including Christians. A very important component for building peace – sharing and coexistence between peoples – is lacking. This is why we are also fighting by encouraging people to remain in front of the facts. We help with humanitarian aid so that people will not be forced to leave their country and their culture. As Christians, we are convinced that we still have a special mission in the Middle East today. We want to be mediators of peace and charity and create bridges of reconciliation between all the parties. We feel as though Pope Francis lived here with us every day. His words and the Church's humanitarian aid (offered to all the population, not only Christians) make us feel that he is very close to us. We feel like Pope Francis is suffering with us, sharing with us. We feel so much compassion, so much solidarity from people all over the world.

6 NOVEMBER 2016[63]

The past few days have been really very hard for our community: 13 of our parishioners were hit by two missiles which fell on their houses in broad daylight. The youngest, 17, may perhaps never walk again. Many children were killed when the missiles fell on the schools and hospitals. We have to continue living this via crucis. Our human logic recognises that there is no solution, no opening of dialogue for a peaceful solution to the Syrian conflict. However, with the eyes of our heart we see that every war that had a beginning also had an end. This has always happened in history. We know that the last word is not that of violence, but of peace, charity and life.

Hope, always

There are signs of hope in Aleppo, even in the drama of the war. With the facts, we Franciscans try to be witnesses of hope. The remaining

63 Homily given during a Mass in the cathedral of Crema

members of the Christian community are witnesses of the fact that the church is very close to those who suffer. It suffers with them and accompanies them at this very difficult moment in which the foundations of the tree are shaken. Its roots are faith, hope and charity, which nourish the lives of people.

For a few years, our humanitarian projects have served all the inhabitants of Aleppo. A great deal of money has been spent to help the people. We spent on a food bank, health expenses, covering the costs for operations and for medicines, repaying mortgages, repairing houses, and distributing drinking water. By sharing the needs of the people we are able to come up with new answers and new ways of coping with need. We try to guess what the Lord wants from us. An Easter hymn springs to my mind. It is often repeated during the Easter vigil and on the following days. *Mors et vita duello conflixere mirando*. There is always war, a struggle between life and death. With the gift of the Spirit, we make life prevail because through his resurrection Jesus has given us the strength of life, the strength to create life even when there is death. So here in Aleppo, in the middle of this city of death, of all the bordering Mediterranean countries which, as Pope Francis said, have become cemeteries, we continue to hope with the force of faith, with the certainty of the heart. It is a continuous conflict, but we have one certainty because God defines himself as the God of the living, the God who created man for life not for death. The God of Abraham, of Isaac and of Jacob is a God of the living and in the end life will prevail. Death for us Christians will always be limited when we look at the real meaning of events, with the simple faith of the people.

9 NOVEMBER 2016[64]

We live in almost impossible conditions; we have not had electricity for more than three years, water is cut off for weeks at a time, 80 per cent of the population is unemployed, 90 per cent of families live below the poverty line and missiles fall everywhere.

In the past 20 days, we have seen a further worsening of the situa-

64   From an interview with *Toscana Oggi*

tion; the failure of the talks at an international level results in an open war without limits, with fighting only a couple of yards away and in which many civilians pay the highest price.

What are we doing as Christians? We Franciscans are the parish priests of all the Latin parishes in Syria. In the western part of the city where the Christian community lives, a missile fell five days ago on a school classroom, leaving six pupils under the rubble, dozens injured and more traumatised. two more missiles fell on a Christian area a few days ago and there too three people were injured and had to have very delicate operations. People have stopped sending their children to school. For the second Sunday we have not been able to hold catechism classes.

Our hope springs from a faithful heart, which is able to look and see the Lord who overcomes death and remains with his suffering people, providing for their needs. This is what I try to convey through letters and messages. I have told the many people who asked me about Aleppo stories of suffering, of the man who has been robbed of his human dignity. But at the same time, I tell of the presence of a tender and merciful God who provides for the needs of the poor who cry out to him.

On the side of the poor

We Franciscans have been in Syria since the thirteenth century, serving as parish priests in all the Latin communities in the territory. We have always worked side by side with the poor during very difficult times in history. Today we continue this pastoral service, which is very important not only for our Latin community but also for all the other Christians and non-Christians who have remained living here. We support 24 humanitarian projects of all types in Aleppo to distribute drinking water, provide minimal electricity for every home, give food parcels to thousands of families and pay for health care for many poor people who could not afford it. Some of our projects concern families, especially young people who decide to get married in this city of death and who, after getting married, want to bring children into the world in Aleppo. We promote small projects for people who do not have work, we support small children from all points of view, guiding their human and spiritual growth. There are many other initiatives inspired by the Holy

Spirit, which continue to come into being. The poor who knock on our door day and night are welcomed and listened to.

Endless dialogue

The war in Aleppo has caused very deep divisions among the people. There is blood, vengeful thoughts, hatred. At the same time, here in western Aleppo, we have managed to keep good relations with all the people who live in our society. Kurds, Druze, Shi'ites and Christians continue to live in peace with one another and are perhaps more supportive than ever, at this time of shared suffering. We see a number of Muslims at funerals and wedding celebrations. Muslims come to our liturgical celebrations, attend holy Mass and listen to the word of God. Communion is always cultivated. At the level of the clergy as well, we have formal (and informal) meetings with all the religious leaders of the other confessions. We meet to talk, sometimes to complain together, and to ask what we can do for the common good of everyone. There is a common nucleus. We Christians, with what we do at the humanitarian level, always try to sew this fabric. We try, with our acts of charity, to stretch out our hand to marginalised, refugee Muslims who have lost homes and loved ones; we always try to build bridges of collaboration to unite all sides into a single human communion.

13 DECEMBER 2016[65]

Gratuitous and disinterested dedication is contagious. Whereas in the beginning my three brothers and I worked alone, almost empty-handed, for some time now we have relied on a large group of volunteers, men and women of all ages, who with moving generosity help us in our daily aid work. In addition, many people in the west are concerned about this martyred people and send us money, with which we can provide for many needs (unfortunately not all of them). We rarely see the major international organisations like the Red Cross or Médecins Sans Frontières.

Our days are characterised by improvisation. Together with the vol-

65 The liberation of the whole city seemed close as the Christian community prepared to celebrate Christmas. From an interview with Cristina Uguccioni (*Vatican Insider*)

unteers, we face the emergencies which come up; we run to help, putting ourselves at the disposal of anyone who needs us. The Christian, as I often repeat, does not only look after his own. We work in many ways. We distribute food parcels, water, clothes and medicine. We help the ill. We look after children, the elderly and the disabled. We repair houses damaged by bombs and help families pay their rent. We dedicate a lot of time to listening to people who are seeking consolation, support and a shoulder to lean on so that they do not feel alone. It is an enormous amount of work. In the frenzied days, which are never the same, we friars always remain anchored to eucharistic celebrations, to prayer, to administering the sacraments. It is Christ who gives us strength and enlarges our hearts to listen to and help this wounded humanity. It is his closeness, his peace and his consolation that we want to bring.

Waiting for the King of Peace

Christmas is a celebration of joy, the birth of the King of Peace who came to offer people his peace. Christmas is a time of great hope, a time of light, the time of liberation from slavery, from prison, time for the freedom of the children of God. In these weeks, we try to convey hope, to bring people the whole message of the birth of the Son: God became man to give every man peace and joy, freedom from evil, what the human being, on his own, cannot give himself. We try to be faithful to the words of John the Baptist who invites us to straighten paths and smooth out rough places so that the Lord can reach people's hearts (Lk 3:4-5). Together with the priests and bishops from other Christian confessions we dedicate a lot of time in this period of Advent to the sacrament of reconciliation, convinced of the immense power of forgiveness. When the waves of hatred and of violence spread, they can end up infecting and hardening people's hearts, compromising family bonds. We encourage everyone to have a merciful gaze upon their dear ones first of all: peace grows out of the peace that keeps families solid and united. We try to offer small but essential signs of hope.

Together with the volunteers, for example, we are involving the children in the building of a large crib that we will place next to the altar. We will organise a moment of celebration for the children, during which we will give them sweets, biscuits and clothes. We want to reach a large number of young people, not only those who usually attend church. So we go to the schools and distribute small gifts. We want them to feel that we are really crossing the threshold of destruction and death to go towards light and life. And then, naturally, we look after adults in many ways.

In the simple daily life that we all live here, signs are understood immediately: when an ill person receives a visit and words of affection accompanied by a blessing full of tenderness, he immediately understands that it is a sign that hope exists. When a very poor family receives the money to cover the costs of giving birth, together with the new baby they will welcome into the world, this is a harbinger of hope. When a boy who has nothing to wear in the winter is given a jacket as a present, he immediately understands the sign and hope is reborn. The same thing happens when a child – who, out of fear, can hardly swallow food – takes part in a celebration (such as the one we organised for St Barbara) and eats a dish of sweetened wheat with his friends. We try to be prophets of hope. In the past few days, we have decorated the church and we have lit lights all around. In the darkness of the night and of hearts, there is the sign of hope and of the light that we are waiting for and which, we are sure, will come.

ADDITIONAL NOTES

ALEPPO BEFORE THE WAR

A *city of coexistence*

It seems incredible today, when we see images of a city devastated by a fratricidal war, but on the eve of conflict in 2012 Aleppo was a city in which coexistence seemed possible. At that time, 2.3 million people lived in the city. Most of them were Sunni Muslims, but there were also many Christians and smaller communities of Shi'ites and Alawites. Not all the Sunni Muslims are Arabs: some are of Kurdish, Turcoman or Circassian origin. The latter, who have Northern European features, are the great-grandchildren of Muslims who in 1865 fled Circassia, a large region on Black Sea that was conquered by Orthodox Russia.

In Aleppo, Muslims and Christians coexisted peacefully and prosperously for many centuries. Before the start of the war the Christian community boasted exemplary numbers; there were 300,000 Christians of all confessions in Aleppo in 2012, comprising one-seventh of the population. The only large Arab cities with a greater number of Christians were Beirut in Lebanon and Cairo in Egypt. Catholics made up almost one-third of the Christians of Aleppo (93,000 according to the Pontifical Yearbook of 2012); 18,000 were Armenian Catholics, 30,000 Chaldeans, 18,000 Greek Melkites, 4,000 Maronites, 10,000 Syrian Catholics and 13,000 Latins (Father Ibrahim's community). The rest of the Christians are divided between the various non-Catholic Churches. The number of Armenians, in particular, is impressive; they number about 60,000, according to data from the Ministry of the Diaspora of the Republic of Armenia. The city is the episcopal see of many Catholic Churches of the Orient (Maronite, Melkite, Syrian Catholic, Armenian Catholic, Chaldean) and of the Catholic vicariate of the Latin church. The bishop of the Latin church Msgr Georges Abou Khazen comes from the Custody of the Holy Land, like Father Ibrahim. In Aleppo, there are at least 12 private schools founded by the Christian community, as well as several hospitals.

In 2012, before the destruction of the city, Aleppo also boasted a number of ancient cathedrals (including the Armenian and Greek Orthodox cathedrals), many churches and parish churches with bell towers rising next to the minarets, a visible and concrete symbol of coexistence. Today, unfortunately, many Christian places of worship have been bombed and are unfit for use.

In 2012, when the war started, there was no Jewish community in Aleppo, but the presence of Jews in the city had been very ancient, certainly preceding that of Christians and Muslims. A precious copy of the Bible, written in Palestine in the tenth century and consulted by the venerated Moses Maimonides 200 years later, is a symbol of the historical vitality of the Jewish community of Aleppo. This book arrived in the city in the thirteenth century, suggesting that the Jewish community of Aleppo was very prosperous. The volume was jealously guarded like a relic for seven centuries in the ancient synagogue of Aleppo. The sacred text was seriously damaged in a fire in the synagogue, during the 1947 attacks on the Jewish community. Living conditions for Jews worsened after 1948, due to a violent anti-Semitic campaign. Their numbers decreased considerably and in 1958 even the ancient Bible followed the flow of Jews fleeing to Jerusalem. The manuscript, known as the Masoretic Aleppo Codex, is now considered the oldest and most complete copy of the Hebrew Bible in existence and it can be seen at the Museum of Israel in Jerusalem.

The centre of trade and industry

Because of its history and beauty, Aleppo was named a UNESCO World Heritage Site. It is one of the very few cities that can claim to have been uninterruptedly inhabited since its foundation which, according to some sources, could have been 2,000 years before Christ.

It was established as a compulsory passage for caravans and merchants on their way from the orient to the west during the Hellenistic period. This is also one of the reasons for the city's periods of economic and cultural prosperity, which over the centuries have kindled appetites and the desire to conquer. It went through destruction by the Persians, siege by the Byzantines, the crusades of Baldwin and was conquered by the Turks of Tamerlane. The situation stabilised when Aleppo became part of the Ottoman Empire and capital of its own province in the sixteenth century, establishing itself as a commercial junction between the Orient and Europe. Its economic importance grew and the Chamber of Commerce of Aleppo was founded in 1885, making it the oldest in the whole of the Middle East. The splendour of the city declined after the First World War, with the division of the Ottoman Empire and the separation of Syria, Turkey and Iraq.

The scenario changed again in the years after Syrian independence, after the Second World War. The city soon became one of the largest industrial centres of the country, rivalling the capital Damascus. Its population went from 300,000 in the 1940s to 2.3 million inhabitants before the present war. In 2011, on the eve of this war, Aleppo was a modern and economically strong city. The University of Aleppo, the second largest university in Syria, had over 60,000 students in 25 faculties. The airport had a capacity of 1.7 million passengers a year, like Rome's Ciampino airport.

Aleppo further reinforced its industrial position in Syria by attracting the majority of foreign productive investment in Syria. This was due, in particular, to some reforms that liberalised the economy in the 1990s. With over 30,000 firms in the city, Aleppo was home to over one-third of Syrian industry and two-thirds of the national textile industry, producing articles in wool and cotton for the whole region. Half of all manufacturing workers in Syria were concentrated in Aleppo. The chemical, pharmaceutical and agro-industrial sectors also developed, as did the electricity, alcoholic beverages, engineering and tourism industries.

The district of Aleppo was also able to negotiate directly with Europe and large financial centres. In the years before the war, entrepreneurs in Aleppo and Turkey were collaborating to transform the area of Jesire, near Aleppo, into an area of economic integration and free trade. The outbreak of the war obviously destroyed all these prospects.

CHRONOLOGY OF THE WAR IN ALEPPO

The so-called "Battle of Aleppo" – the clash between the regular army and anti-government militia – started late in July 2012, 16 months after the start of the fighting in the rest of the country.

It was immediately clear to everyone that Aleppo held the balance of power in this conflict. Winning this rich and strategic city, the economic engine and cultural and multi-religious centre that was Aleppo, would be equivalent to appropriating the heart of the country and possibly winning the war. This explains the bloody tenacity shown by both sides during the five terrible years of war.

The composition of both sides – supporters of President Bashar al-Assad and his opponents – has definitely changed over the years. Assad on one side has obtained the military support of the Lebanese Shi'ite movement Hezbollah, of the Iranian armed forces and, lastly, of the Russian air force and army. On the other side, the militias that oppose the regime are supported by a US-headed international coalition called Friends of Syria and have certainly changed their colour. Many of the fighters were initially inspired by lay ideals of freedom and justice. With the passing of time, however, and the arrival of fundamentalist militias from many regions of the world (from Tunisia to Bosnia, from Chechnya to Saudi Arabia and Europe) and above all with the advent of the so-called Islamic State, the opposition to Assad increasingly took on the appearance of a threatening and violent Islamist force, far from any democratic principle and from the ideal of guaranteeing minorities and respecting their religious freedom.

2012: *the beginning of the end*

In May 2012, the protests against President Bashar al-Assad also began in Aleppo. On 19 July the first armed conflicts took place between the army and anti-government forces in Salaheddine, a neighbourhood south of the city that was famous for its football stadium. Explosions and artillery strikes continued over the following days. The rebels, who came from the nearby rural area, proclaimed the start of the battle for the liberation of Aleppo and entered the city in large numbers.

In August, the rebels established a strategic checkpoint north of Aleppo to control the routes of communication between the city and the border with Turkey.

2013-2014: *the conflict continues*

Between December 2012 and January 2013, the activities of the international airport of Aleppo were stopped because of fighting and the city became even more isolated. The city's cultural heritage began to suffer; rebels attacked the historic mosque of the Omayyads, a monument of incredible value.

In June 2013, the Syrian army supported by Hezbollah started a counter-offensive, the so-called "North Storm Operation", to regain the lost territories of the city. Despite great deployments of forces, the rebels resisted. From October 2013 until November 2014, government forces tightened the siege on the neighbourhoods of Aleppo that were in the hands of the rebels. In June 2014, the Islamic State proclaimed the birth of the Caliphate; it confirmed the worrying growth of the Islamic fundamentalist wing in the rebel front. As a consequence, Aleppo also became one of the objectives of the so-called Islamic State. In November 2014, the United Nations proposed that the Syrian army should let the rebels leave Aleppo unharmed on condition that they give up their weapons. The Free Syrian Army refused the proposal.

2015: *war of attrition*

The year started with an offensive by the rebels, who gained more ground in the city. In mid-February, the Syrian army moved its troops to the north of Aleppo with the objective of cutting off routes to the rebels in the city. After a consistent advance, however, the offensive stopped and the rebels regained ground.

On 15 June, in preparation for a new offensive, the rebels heavily bombed the areas of Aleppo that were in the hands of government forces, leaving dozens dead and almost 200 injured. Also in June, the rebels conquered the Centre for Scientific Research of Aleppo, where there was a barracks of the Syrian army. The Syrian army's counter-offensive failed. At the end of September, Russia entered the war in support of Bashar al-Assad and started to bomb the rebels' targets.

In the middle of October, the Islamic State entered the scene near Aleppo, capturing four villages which until that moment had been governed by other rebel forces. At the end of December, however, the Syrian army advanced and, with the aid of Hezbollah, managed to gain control of a large area south of the city.

2016: the city on its knees

According to internal sources, the population of greater Aleppo (encompassing the city and its suburbs) shrunk to about 1.5 million by 2016. Those who could, fled, losing everything: their work, homes and friends.

In early February, the regular army with the Russian air force and Hezbollah won back several villages north of the city, strategic positions which allowed them to control the routes of communication between Aleppo and Turkey. In this way, they tried to prevent supplies and men from reaching the rebels left in the city.

At the end of February, rebel forces advanced to the south of Aleppo, conquering a number of villages and strategic routes of communication between the city and the south of the country. However, the government launched a counter-offensive, winning back control of the territory.

In June, the Syrian army and its allies started a crucial campaign called "Operation Castle" aimed at winning a stretch of the motorway north-west of Aleppo that was in the hands of the rebels. This road linked the territories controlled by the rebels to the outside and inside of the city. Winning this route of communication would mean isolating the rebel parts of Aleppo and being able to tighten the siege. At the end of July, the operation was successful.

Russian and government troops immediately proposed opening humanitarian corridors to evacuate civilians from the rebel-held areas under siege, as the rebels prepared for a counter-offensive.

At the end of October, the rebels tried to win back some positions to break the siege around the occupied quarters in the eastern part of the city. After an initial success, they were defeated by the superiority of their opponents' men, weapons and materials. In the second half of November, Syrian loyalist troops began an offensive on east Aleppo. They were supported by heavy bombing by the Russians, who are believed to have made use of cluster bombs, as well as by Iran and the Shi'ite militia of Hezbollah. The few hospitals still working were bombed and rendered unusable, just like the civil infrastructures. Between 26 and 28 November, the northern part of Aleppo east (about one-third of the territory controlled by the rebels) was won back by the government forces, causing the flight of more than 10,000 civilians. At the end of a fruitless counter-offensive by the rebels, the government, Russian and Shi'ite forces launched a last attack on the pocket still controlled by the rebels.

On the evening of 7 December, the troops of Damascus regained possession of the old city of Aleppo, including the ancient citadel. Between 15 and 22 December – amid many difficulties and tensions – the last rebel fighters, their families and the civilians who did not want to leave the areas which had returned under government control, were evacuated towards Idlib. Aleppo was declared a "safe city".

THE HISTORY OF THE CUSTODY IN SYRIA:

A FAITHFUL PRESENCE SINCE 1200

The Franciscan presence in Syria has eight centuries of history. The oldest source that confirms the activity of friars in Aleppo is a document signed by Pope Gregory IX on 7 June 1238. The letter is addressed to 110 Templar Knights and several other Christians imprisoned by the Saracens and locked up in the citadel of the city. The Pope helped them receive confession and communion from either a Friar named Manasserio, probably of French origin, or another Friar Minor of Aleppo.

Since the sixteenth century, the Franciscans in the city looked after the spiritual life of the European colony in Aleppo, made up of mostly Venetian merchants. In 1645 the monastery and church of the Franciscans were destroyed by the Turks. The friars nevertheless stayed in the city. They overcame countless difficulties and in the eighteenth century opened a new church from which to continue their work. In 1824, a devastating earthquake destroyed the monastery. The friars again decided to stay. In the second half of the nineteenth century, the Franciscans moved to the area of Azizieh, a popular area among Aleppo's Christians. The Franciscans still live there today. In 1934 the church of St Francis, the parish where Fra Ibrahim and his brothers work, was built.

Today, there are about 15 Franciscans in Syria carrying out their mission in various cities.

They operate in the monastery of St Paul Apostle in Damascus, near the sanctuary of St Ananias, dedicated to the Christian man the Lord ordered to host Paul after his conversion (Acts 9:3-4). In Aleppo, the Franciscans work in the Latin parish of St Francis of Assisi in Azizieh, in the parish branch in Er-Ram and in the College of the Holy Land, which is in the western part of the city.

In the coastal city of Latakia, they live in the monastery of the Sacred

Heart of Jesus. They carry out an activity of exceptional value in some villages in the valley of the Orontes, in the north of the country (Ghassanieh, Yacoubieh, Knayeh). Islamic militias have been governing this area for a few years. The situation is extremely dangerous and, in 2016, two friars were kidnapped by the militia before being providentially released. These risks have made the Custody return to the question of whether to leave Syria or remain.

This is how Msgr Pierbattista Pizzaballa, then Custos of the Holy Land, answered these doubts and fears in early 2016: "The Custody has never abandoned the places and the population that the church has entrusted to it, even at the risk of danger. Quite a few of our martyrs, have died in circumstances that are not too dissimilar from those of the current situation. A shepherd does not abandon his flock and does not ask whether his sheep are worth a lot or little, whether there are a lot of them or whether they are young. For a shepherd, all his sheep are important and he loves them all in the same way."

The friars of the Custody are still in Syria with their Christians.

SUPPORT FOR FRANCISCAN FRIARS AND

ATS PRO TERRA SANCTA

"With deep concern I am following the dramatic circumstances of the civilian populations involved in the violent conflicts in beloved Syria [...] I hope that with generous solidarity, the necessary help is given to them in order to secure their survival and dignity" (Pope Francis, 7 February 2016)

The Friars of the Custody of the Holy Land have faithfully remained in Syria throughout the war. They are present in a number of cities: Latakia, Damascus, Aleppo and a few villages in the Oronte valley. They help the local population, paying particular attention to women and children and making no distinctions between people. They have created four reception centres, supported by ATS pro Terra Sancta, to provide for food, clothing and basic necessities. They also try to cope with the healthcare emergency with basic medical services provided by the Aleppo hospital run by the Custody and by distributing medicines through dispensaries in the monasteries.

How you can support the work of the Franciscans in Syria

Six years on from the beginning of the war Aleppo is still in great need of food, milk for children, clothes, medicines and medical equipment. People whose houses were destroyed by bombs are also urgently in need of help, as are those who cannot pay their children's school or university fees. You can be close to the Franciscan friars in Syria through ATS pro Terra Sancta.

Donations, which are promptly transferred to the friars in Syria, can be made by:

BANK TRANSFER
ATS - Associazione di Terra Santa
Banca Popolare Etica - **IBAN: IT67 W050 18121010 0000 0122691**
BIC CODE: CCRTIT2T84A

ONLINE
By credit card or PayPal, at **www.proterrasancta.org**